In Her Wake

Frances Elizabeth Roads Elliott
1852-1924

by
Sharon S. Atkins

Photo: Frances Elizabeth Roads Elliott
Courtesy of Tom Elliott

Also by Sharon S. Atkins

www.sharonsatkins.com

*Word of mouth is an author's best friend.
If you enjoyed reading any of the listed, your review at Amazon will be most appreciated.*

With a Heart for Any Fate: Hazel's Memoir

How the Stars Aligned in 69:
Historical Context for the Founding of P.E.O.

The P.E.O. Founders' Scrapbook

Ephemera: Genealogy Gold

Cemetery Research

Understanding U.S. Vital Records

Unraveling Brick Wall Mysteries

In Her Wake

Frances Elizabeth Roads Elliott
1852-1924

by
Sharon S. Atkins

©2017, copyright Sharon S. Atkins. All rights reserved.

All rights reserved. No part of this book may be reproduced in any form whatsoever, whether by graphic, visual, electronic, film, microfilm, tape recording, or any other means, without prior written permission of the publisher, except in the case of brief passages embodied in critical reviews and articles.

The opinions and views expressed herein belong solely to the author. Permission for the use of sources, graphics, and photos is also solely the responsibility of the author.

Front cover image courtesy of Big Stock Photos.

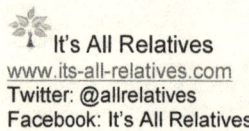 It's All Relatives
www.its-all-relatives.com
Twitter: @allrelatives
Facebook: It's All Relatives

Acknowledgements

A special thank-you is due to the descendants of Frances Elizabeth Roads Elliott and Simon Charles Elliott who so graciously shared their family stories, memories and photos with me to help bring this story to life; especially Chris Canfield, Jane Elliott, Tom Elliott and Ann Weisberg.

*This book is dedicated with lots of Grandma hugs to three boys who bring sunshine into my life:
A.C., Brady and Dane.*

Table of Contents

Acknowledgements 7
Foreword 13
   Introduction 17
Chapter 1: Before Iowa Wesleyan 1852 – 1866 21
   McClure Ancestors 22
   Roads Ancestors 23
   Addison Roads Family 25
   Howe's Academy 28
   Civil War 31
Chapter 2: 1866-1872 33
   History of Iowa Wesleyan 33
   Franc's Iowa Wesleyan and Post-Graduate Education 35
   Simon Charles Elliott 37
Chapter 3: 1872-1893 49
   Life in Nebraska for Franc 1872-1893 49
   Elliott's Land Transactions 67
   Simon C. Elliott and His Store 68
   Phebe Leech Elliott 72
   Lincoln, Nebraska Historical Perspective 78
Chapter 4: 1893-1903 81
   Canfield and Elliott Families 81
   Elliot Family and University of Nebraska Relationships 88
   Franc R. Elliott: 1893-1903 93
   1894-1898: Aurora, Illinois 94
   1898-1903: Salt Lake City Public Schools 96
   Simon C. Elliott and the Extended Elliott Family: 1893-1903 126
Chapter 5: 1903-1915 131
   Simon C. Elliott and Extended Family: 1903-1915 141
Chapter 6: 1915-1924 149
   Extended Elliott Family 158
Chapter 7: After Franc 167
   Franc and Simon's Son: Dr. Charles Addison Elliott (1873-1939) 167
   Franc and Simon's Daughter-in-Law: Genevieve Comstock
      Cole Elliott (1889-1965) 169
   Franc and Simon's Grandson: Frank Roads Elliott (1913-1974) 170
   Franc and Simon's Granddaughter: Margaret C. Elliott (1914-1996) ...171
   Franc and Simon's Grandson: Ernest Charles Elliott (1920-1993) 172
   Franc and Simon's Daughter: Stella Mae Elliott
      Canfield (1843-1947) 173

Franc and Simon's Son-in-Law: James A. Canfield (1874-1959).........174
Franc and Simon's Grandson: Charles Elliott Canfield (1900-1973)....174
Franc and Simon's Grandson: Robert Elliott Canfield (1903-1980) 175

Roads and Elliott Ancestors 177
Photographs 183
Bibliography 201
About the Author..213

Foreword

Upon the occasion of the dedication of a memorial stone in the Forest Home cemetery for Frances Elizabeth Roads Elliott, one of the seven founders of the Philanthropic Educational Organization (P.E.O.) Sisterhood - referred to on the stone as Franc Roads Elliott.

"Today, we are remembering by a very small stone, one who was to us a great woman, who unconsciously to herself and perhaps to us here today set the pattern for P.E.O. philanthropies since her activities were in the field of education and in civic service, particularly in the advancement of women, politically and in her participation in the affairs of the church."

Mrs. Mabel Scurrah of Victoria, B.C.
Supreme Chapter president [1]

Photo: Tombstone located at Forest Home Cemetery, Mount Pleasant, Henry, Iowa. Photo found at Find-A-Grave.com submitted by Anonymous

---

[1] "Memorial to One of P.E.O. Founders Dedicated." *Mount Pleasant News* (Mt. Pleasant, Iowa), 29 Sep 1952:1.

Frances Elizabeth Roads Elliott
1852-1924

Photo: Frances Elizabeth Roads Elliott
Courtesy of Tom Elliott

Introduction

In early 2014, while researching the lives of the seven founders of the Philanthropic Educational Organization (P.E.O.) Sisterhood, the thought to tell a fuller story of Franc Roads' life began to tug at me. The result of my initial research evolved into "The P.E.O. Founders' Scrapbook." Parts of that research evolved to become the seeds which grew into this book.

Even as I was compiling the stories for each of the seven for "The P.E.O. Founders' Scrapbook," it occurred to me that there was a lot more to learn about each of them; Mary Allen, Alice Bird, Hattie Briggs, Alice Coffin, Suela Pearson, Franc Roads and Ella Stewart. Together they founded the P.E.O. Sisterhood, however, individually each was an accomplished woman in her own right.

After "The P.E.O. Founders' Scrapbook" was published, I tucked the thought of writing more in depth individual stories away. I knew to do justice to each of these women, it would be a massive effort to research, compile and write their individual stories. I also knew the right time to approach such a project would come along one day.

Since 2014, I have performed limited research to develop entertaining posts for the Facebook page dedicated to "The P.E.O. Founders' Scrapbook." To date, the compiled list, by founder, of all the posts published is approximately 120 pages.

The amount of information relating to Franc began to pile up to the point where it became evident it is time to tell Franc's story.

While we can admire Franc for the role she plays in the founding of the P.E.O. Sisterhood, she accomplishes so much more in her lifetime than that one defining moment.

She is a brilliant student, a devoted daughter, a partner to her husband, a mother to her children, a member of an extended family and a fierce advocate for women and their abilities within their communities. She never stops attending classes or continuing to learn. She expands her own mind as well as the minds of her students.

As you read this story about Franc and her life, keep in mind what was happening in the rest of the country, indeed her world, during her lifetime: 1852-1924. Consider her actions, decisions and motivations in context of her time, her era.

The following list may help. Some of this list is a subset of the "United States History Timeline 9200-2015," developed by Eric Davis and found at http://hopes-and-dreams.net.

1852:	Harriet Beecher Stowe publishes Uncle Tom's Cabin
1854:	Florence Nightingale sent to Crimean War
1857:	Dred Scott decision: slaves did not become free in a free state
1860-1861:	Pony Express service starts and ends
1861:	Transcontinental telegraph service begins
1861-1865:	Civil War
1862:	Homestead Act
1863:	Emancipation Proclamation

1865:	President Abraham Lincoln assassinated
1867:	Alaska purchased from Russia
1869:	Wyoming approves and grants women's suffrage
1869:	Elizabeth Cady Stanton is first woman to testify before Congress
1869:	Completion of the Transcontinental Railroad
1869:	Suez Canal opens
1869:	Heinz food company founded by Henry John Heinz
1870:	15th Amendment grants African-American men right to vote
1871:	Chicago fire
1872:	C.A. Pillsbury and Company founded by Charles Alfred and John S. Pillsbury.
1873:	Susan B. Anthony votes for President and fined $100
1873:	P.T. Barnum's "Greatest Show on Earth" first appears in NYC
1876:	Beginning of Bell telephone
1876:	Mark Twain publishes Tom Sawyer
1878:	Thomas Edison starts electric company
1886:	Invention of Coca-Cola
1886:	Geronimo surrenders
1886:	Dedication of the Statue of Liberty
1890:	General Electric starts
1890:	Wounded Knee massacre
1892:	Ellis Island opens to immigrants

1892:	Pledge of Allegiance first recited in public schools
1897:	Invention of Campbell's soup
1898:	Annexation of Hawaii
1898:	Spanish-American War
1901:	President William McKinley assassinated
1901:	Picasso experiences first major exhibition of his artwork
1901:	Big oil discovery in Texas
1903:	Ford Motor Company starts
1903:	Wright brothers plane flies
1906:	San Francisco earthquake
1908:	General Motors starts
1910:	Boy Scouts founded
1912:	Titanic sinks
1914:	Panama Canal opens
1914-1918:	World War I
1915:	Movie "Birth of a Nation" debuts
1915:	Lusitania sinks
1917-1933:	Prohibition
1920:	19th Amendment passes - Women vote
1923:	Time Magazine starts
1923:	Walt Disney Company founded

I hope you enjoy learning about Franc Roads Elliott. And come to agree not only was Franc far ahead of her time, but we are all still following, to some degree or another, as Winona Reeves states in 1919, *In Her Wake*.

Chapter 1: Before Iowa Wesleyan 1852 – 1866

"It is indeed gratifying that from seven the organization numbers 10,000, organized women holding within their circle, latent dynamic possibilities for good. The older I grow the more firmly I believe that the social and economic problems of the day will be solved by organized womanhood."

Franc Roads Elliott,
P.E.O. 1907 International Convention

To understand the scope of the life of Frances Elizabeth Roads, known as Franc to her family and friends, it's best to start back at the beginning; 10 February 1852. Franc's parents, Addison Roads and Nancy McClure Roads, marry 7 March 1849 in Hendricks County, Indiana; about three years before Franc, their first child, is born.

The 1917 Iowa Wesleyan College Historical Sketch and Alumni Record reports Franc's place of birth as "near Marshall" Iowa. Today, there is no town in Iowa named Marshall; only Marshalltown in Marshall County, Iowa. Today, Marshalltown is approximately 135 miles northwest of Mt. Pleasant, where the P.E.O. Sisterhood is founded in 1869. It's originally named Marshall in 1853 by the first settler, Henry Anson; a year after Franc's birth. Mr. Anson names the location Marshall after Marshall, Michigan, where he previously lived. Marshall County, Iowa forms six years prior to Franc's birth in 1846 and is named for fourth Chief Justice of the United States Supreme Court John Marshall.

At the time of Franc's birth in 1852, Iowa has been a state for six years. Millard Fillmore is serving as the 13th President of the United States and Stephen P. Hempstead is Governor of Iowa.

It is reasonable to conclude Franc's parents meet in Hendricks County, Indiana. The 1840 census records list both the Roads and McClure families living in the area. It is also plausible Franc is named for her maternal grandmother, Frances McClure.

McClure Ancestors

The Elliott family history, compiled by Dr. Frank Roads Elliott and Thomas Elliott, relates William McClure, Franc's maternal grandfather, at age 19, serves in the War of 1812, under General Andrew Jackson. "He was one of the rifleman who defeated the British at the Battle of New Orleans. He was discharged at Mobile, and walked to his home plantation in Tennessee, 1100 miles. Fifteen men started with him on that long hike through swamp, wilderness and mountains, a trail beset by fever, hunger, outlaws and the deadly peril of Indians. Of the 15 men who started, McClure and one other survived. One day when their shoes had worn out and they had tied the remnants on the bottoms of their feet, one soldier was so much distressed he sat down on a stump to rest. When Colonel Balue ordered him to proceed, he tried to rise but failed, then the Colonel struck him over the shoulders with his sword. The man staggered a few steps and fell dead. His comrades wished for one more battle or an excuse to have revenge on such a brutal officer."

According to the "History of Hendricks County" (Indiana), William McClure is a native of Virginia and migrates to Hendricks County, Indiana in the spring of 1830 with his wife, Frances Rose McClure. Together they have eleven children; Franc's mother, Nancy, being their fifth child is born near Rogersville, Tennessee.

William McClure and his wife, Frances, are listed in the 1850 Census as living in Liberty, Hendricks, Indiana. However, in May of 1850, Frances McClure dies and in October the same year, William McClure is killed by Indians while hauling logs.

One of Nancy's brothers, Charles Wesley McClure, marries Edna Hiatt in 1851. Charles and Edna migrate to Iowa where they live until 1856. They return to Indiana after 1856 to spend the rest of their lives in Hendricks County. Charles and Edna, with their daughters, are living in Jefferson, Henry County, Iowa at the time of both the 1854 and 1856 Iowa Census. One of their daughters, Franc's cousin Elizabeth McClure, is born in Henry County, Iowa in 1852.

Roads Ancestors

Biographies about Addison Road's family identify records for Addison's great-grandfather as Valentine Roth. Valentine is born about 1708 in Germany. He migrates from Germany to Pennsylvania in September 1743.

One of Valentine's children is Addison's grandfather, Abraham Roth/Rode, born in Pennsylvania in 1750. Abraham's baptismal record, dated 18 Mar 1750, is from the Great Swamp Reformed Congregational Church in Lower Milford Township, Lehigh, Pennsylvania. Within

Pennsylvania records, the surnames Roth and Roads are used interchangeably.

Evidence found in Mennonite Vital records suggest Abraham moves his family to Shenandoah County from Lancaster County, Pennsylvania sometime prior to 1785. Addison's father, George Roads, is born in 1785 in Virginia. Abraham and his brothers Jacob and John patent a tract of 251 acres in Shenandoah County, Virginia in 1789. The Elliott family history, compiled by Dr. Frank Roads Elliott and Thomas Elliott, reports George Roads was ten years of age before he could speak English. As with many immigrants of this era, the family keeps strong ties with their native language. This history also states George is blind in one eye.

Abraham sells this property and moves to Rockbridge County, Virginia in the 1790's and then migrates to Highland County, Ohio about 1805. Franc's grandfather, George, goes to Ohio as well – he was about 20 years old at the time.

George Roads remains in Ohio, where he marries Mary Elizabeth Boyd. Their son, Addison, is born in 1825.

Many of the Roads family descendants are buried in Highland County, Ohio at either Roads Cemetery, Highland Cemetery, Old Dutch Cemetery or Buford Cemetery.

According to the Federal Census data, we are aware Addison Roads' father, George, is in Indiana by 1840. This data confirms the Elliott family history compiled by Dr. Frank Roads Elliott and Thomas Elliott, stating George and family migrate to Hendricks County in 1836.

This Elliott family history, states that as a boy, Addison attends country school in Ohio, until he moves to Indiana. Once in Indiana, he only attends school in the winter time, paying his way by working between times.

Addison's father, George Roads, is also listed on the 1850 Census in Liberty, Hendricks, Indiana.

In 1850, the William McClure family and the George Roads family are listed on the same Census page. William's daughter, Nancy, and George Roads son, Addison, are neighbors when they marry in 1849.

Interestingly, Nancy McClure's oldest brother, Arthur A. McClure, marries Mary Jane Roads, a younger sibling to Addison Roads, on 27 Dec 1843; a little over five years before Franc's parents marry in Hendricks County, Indiana.

Addison Roads Family

Born in Hillsborough, Highland County, Ohio in 1825, Franc's father, Addison Roads, relocates with his family in 1836 from Ohio to Hendricks County, Indiana.

Addison Roads marries Nancy McClure on 7 March 1849. It is a rainy day according to the Elliott family history. Within the 1850 Census, taken eighteen months before Franc's birth, Addison Roads, lists his occupation as a blacksmith. He and his wife, Nancy, are living in Liberty Township, Hendricks, Indiana; the same town as their parents.

Sometime between August 1850, the date of the 1850 census, and February 1852 when Franc is born, Addison and Nancy move 350 miles due west from Liberty Township to Wayland, Henry County, Iowa.

In 1851, Addison's sister, Julia, marries William A. Jessup, who is a farmer in Hendricks County, Indiana. William and his brother, Jonathan, first locate in Jefferson Township, Henry County Iowa in 1849. According to "Portrait and Biographical Album of Henry County," the rest of his Jessup family follow William in 1850. They arrive in Henry County that spring. In 1851, William is elected as Township Clerk of Jefferson Township, Henry, Iowa and in 1852 as Township Trustee. During his career, William also serves as a County Supervisor and as a Justice.

Addison and Nancy's married siblings, Arthur McClure and Mary Jane Roads McClure, are also listed in the 1850 Census living in the town of Jefferson, Henry County, Iowa. Arthur cites being a farmer.

It is quite possible Franc's parents, Addison and Nancy Roads, are enticed to move to Henry County, Iowa by family members. Perhaps Addison's sisters, Mary Jane and her husband Arthur McClure; and Julia and her husband William Jessup convince the young couple to move to Henry County.

By 1852, when Franc is born, Nancy McClure Roads' siblings Charles, William and Arthur; and Addison's siblings, Mary Jane and Julie, are all living in Henry County, Iowa (where Mt. Pleasant is located); as well as Addison and Nancy Roads.

In the winter of 1855, the Addison Roads family moves to Mt. Pleasant, Henry County, Iowa.

Sometime prior to 1856, Nancy's sister Katharine, and her husband Gideon Potts, also move from Indiana to Henry County, Iowa.

The first documented evidence for Franc is the 1856 Iowa State Census. Again, Addison identifies his occupation as a blacksmith. Living with him are Nancy and Frances E., who is 5 years old. This Census record indicates the family is living in Center Township, Henry County, Iowa. Center Township contains the town of Mt. Pleasant.

Also living with the Roads family are two students, William H. Chauncy and W.C. Courtright. They are boarders living with the Roads family and are conceivably attending an educational institution in the area.

Franc's younger brother, Charles A. Roads, is born in 1859 when she is about five years of age.

By the time of the 1860 Census, the Roads family has expanded to include both Franc and her brother Charles. Charles is listed as two years old. Frances is age 9. Their father, Addison, states his occupation is as a grocer.

One of the last records found for Franc's brother, Charles, is the 1880 Census. At that time, he is living with his parents at age 21 and claims his occupation as a civil engineer with the railroad.

On 3 December 1854, Leona Katherine Potts Roads is born in Indiana to Katherine McClure and Gideon Potts. Katherine McClure Potts is an older sister to Franc's mother Nancy. Thus, Leona is a first cousin to Franc. By the time Leona is 16 years old, in 1870, both of her parents are deceased and she is found living with Addison and Nancy Roads. All records associated with Leona from that point on, refer to her as the daughter of Addison and Nancy. Leona's marriage license, dated 7 October 1886, lists her name as Leona Roads.

At age 43, Leona marries a widower, Henry Bowman. She becomes step-mother to three young daughters, Gertrude, age 11; Florence, age 8; and Mary Frances, age 6.

The Elliott family history, compiled by Dr. Frank Roads Elliott and Thomas Elliott reports during the Civil War Addison Roads is a *Sutler* with the Iowa Cavalry in Missouri for seven months. A Sutler is a merchant who follows the armies to sell merchandise to soldiers. According to Wikipedia, frequently Sutlers are the only local suppliers of non-military goods. This information is supported by Civil War draft records, dated June 1863, listing Addison, age 38, as a Sutler in 1st Iowa Cavalry.

The *Burlington Weekly Hawk-Eye* newspaper reports in March of 1865 on recent elections in Mt. Pleasant. M.L. Edwards is elected Mayor, and the Councilmen from the Third Ward are reported to be Reuben Allen and A. Roads; fathers of Mary Allen and Franc Roads, who four years later are two of the co-founders of the P.E.O. Sisterhood.

Franc is surrounded by family while growing up in Mt. Pleasant. Between her aunt Mary Jane Roads, sibling to her father, Addison, who married Arthur, a sibling to her mother, Nancy; and, her aunt Julia Ann Roads Jessup and Julie's husband William, also sibling to her father, Addison, there are a dozen or more cousins growing up in Mt. Pleasant at the same time.

Howe's Academy

From the book "Out of the Heart," we learn Franc attends Howe's Academy before she enters Iowa Wesleyan in

September 1866 at the age of 14. Thus, it is conceivable she is a student at Howe's Academy from about 1857 to 1866.

The following story is derived from "Story of the 'Old Mill' As Told by a Howe" in the *Mount Pleasant News*. The story, dated 11 September 1936, is written by the W.P. Howe, son of the founder of Howe's Academy. According to this story, the founder of Howe's Academy, Professor Samuel Luke Howe, made the 700-mile trek from Ohio to Iowa with his family in two-horse wagons in 1841.

In 1842, Professor Samuel Howe begins teaching in a little log cabin on his farm; specifically set aside for that purpose.

Professor Howe moves his school to a location in the upper room of the old log jail in Mt. Pleasant in 1843. By 1844, the school again re-locates; this time to the Cumberland Presbyterian Church building. Afterwards, Howe's school moves to the residence of Dr. Wellington Bird. Dr. Bird is father to another of the P.E.O. founders, Alice Bird.

During the summer of 1845, Professor Howe completes construction of a four-story academic building which can accommodate "easily the neighborhood of hundred pupils. The school also receives the name of 'Old Mill.'" The name being given by its enemies as a term of derision. Instead, this name becomes a term of endearment by those who attend.

In 1848, Professor Howe becomes a stock holder in the only abolitionist newspaper published in the "great-west," the *Iowa Freeman*. Initially published at Fort Madison, the paper moves to Mt. Pleasant in 1849. Howe continues to teach and run the school, as well as manage the newspaper. The newspaper is never a profit-making venture; but, a passion for its owner.

In 1850, Professor Howe becomes President of the First County Teachers' Association, which is organized at Mt. Pleasant.

Professor Howe is also connected with Iowa Wesleyan University. He is one of the faculty members of the college at the same time as James Harlan; who later becomes a U.S. Senator. In 1868, Harlan also becomes father-in-law to Robert Todd Lincoln, son of Abraham Lincoln.

According to Sandy Williams, in an article about the school, found in the 11 November 1972 edition of the *Mount Pleasant News*, "Pioneer education was almost a luxury. There were no public schools and no compulsory education.... But with the Howes (Samuel and his son, Seward) in charge, education was exciting and challenging. No arbitrary rules of conduct existed. Freedom of personal conduct, shocking to the Victorian ideas prevalent at the time, prevailed. The school had no fixed hours or rules of study. The only requirement was to master certain subjects by diligent study."

After Professor Samuel Howe's death in 1877, his son Seward Curtis Howe acts as head of Howe's Academy. The article referenced also mentions that Seward's wife, Mary Evelyn Glenny Howe, was a P.E.O. member.

Howe's Academy ultimately closes in 1916 due to declining enrollment.

Civil War

When the Civil War begins in April of 1861, Franc was 9 years old.

According to the Iowa Pathway's story, "Iowa in the Civil War," "the state of Iowa has thousands of soldiers who volunteer to serve. Initially, the soldiers are fighting to prevent the southern states from leaving the Union. After the Emancipation Proclamation in 1862 declares slaves will be free, not all in Iowa support the law. However, by the end of war, most Iowa soldiers wanted to see an end to slavery."

Mt. Pleasant, located approximately 30 miles from the Mississippi River, and near the roads and Indian trails created during the 1830's-1850's, has ties to the Freedom Trail and Underground Railroad. Slaves, on the run to freedom, come through Iowa from Missouri, Kansas and Nebraska using these paths to reach the northeast or Canada.

One of the changes brought about by war is that women became teachers. Prior to the war most school teachers are men; but women fill in while the men become soldiers. Once the war is over, women continue to teach school and within a short time period most teachers are women.

Franc's father, Addison, age 36 at the start of the War, does not appear to have served as a soldier, but as a Sutler as previously mentioned. Franc's future husband, Simon Charles Elliott serves in the Union army; as well as two of her uncles, George W. McClure and James H. McClure.

In the summer of 1864, Simon answers President Lincoln's call to be one of the Hundred Days Men; which are men recruited during an all-out recruitment effort by the Union Army to have enough soldiers to end the war in 100 days. Simon joins the 45th Iowa Infantry and is assigned to Company A. Company A is primarily comprised of volunteers from Henry County, Iowa. Reuben Allen, father to P.E.O. founder Mary Allen, also enlists in Company A of the 45th Iowa Infantry.

Simon's military records indicate he spends one month of his 100 days service in the hospital of a military camp near Memphis, Tennessee. The regiment, organized in Keokuk, Iowa, first travels to St. Louis, then Memphis and Moscow, Tennessee. They are assigned to the duty of guarding the Memphis camp for the Charleston Railroad until they all muster out in September 1864. The Memphis and Charleston Railroad becomes of great strategic importance during the War, as it was the only east-west railroad that runs through Confederate States. According to Wikipedia, a total of 972 men serve in the 45th regiment during its existence.

During the War, many Union soldiers come through Mt. Pleasant on their way to camp Harlan, just west of the town.

When the war ends in April 1865, over 76,500 Iowa men serve in the Iowa Union army. In fact, according to Wikipedia, "Iowa sent more soldiers to the Civil War than any other state." Over 13,000 from Iowa die, more from disease than combat.

Chapter 2: 1866-1872

"Franc Rhodes (sic) was the girl with the far vision, and she was so progressive that she might have been set down in a college twenty-five years ahead of her time and not had to hasten her step to keep abreast. She was artistic and very beautiful, as her girlhood picture shows. No P.E.O. in the thirty thousand is one lap ahead of her today, and most of us are far in her wake."

Winona Reeves, The Story of P.E.O., 1919

History of Iowa Wesleyan

The "Historical Sketch and Alumni Record of Iowa Wesleyan College," published in 1917 states:

"In 1841, when Mt. Pleasant was but a hamlet of a few humble cottages, such men as I.I. Stewart, Peter Smith, E. Killpatrick, J.C. Hall, P.C. Tiffany, Samuel Nelson, Nelson Lathrop, John P. Grantham, and a score of others, 'whose names are as ointment poured forth,' in the memory of those days, were suggesting, counseling, planning, hoping, daring, and in 1842 meeting with the people en masse to discuss the relation of the hopes and future prosperity of the young territory to higher education. Of this labor of brain and heart Iowa Wesleyan was brought forth, first of all the educational institutions of her grade in Iowa, and first of all such institutions in the country on the west of the Mississippi."

As stated in the book, "The P.E.O. Founders' Scrapbook," with the promise of a free education for veteran soldiers, the end of the Civil War brings many men to Iowa Wesleyan. It is believed these soldiers could add breath and new life into the school, and to Mt. Pleasant, which suffers financial hardships during the War. The freshman class of 1865 names themselves the Lifebloods, to symbolize what they mean to the school and the community.

Entering Iowa Wesleyan in the fall of 1866, Franc did not enter Iowa Wesleyan with those freshman, but she completes her courses in three years; ending up with the Lifebloods graduating class of 1869.

It was only ten years before Franc enters Iowa Wesleyan, in 1856, when the first college-level graduate, Winfield Scott Mayne graduates from Iowa Wesleyan with a Bachelor of Arts degree.

Almost from the beginning, Iowa Wesleyan promotes opportunities for women in education. In 1859, Lucy Webster Killpatrick is the first woman to graduate. Interestingly, Franc's future father-in-law, Charles Elliott, is the President of the institution in 1859. Franc's future sister-in-law, Phebe Leech Elliott, graduates in 1860. She becomes a Professor of English Literature and Preceptors 1864-1865. She also serves as a member of the Board of Trustees at Iowa Wesleyan from 1870-1875.

In the spring of 1866, Arabella (Belle) Babb graduates with a law degree from Iowa Wesleyan and becomes the first woman to be admitted to the bar in the United States. In 1873, Bella's brother, Washington Irving Babb marries another founder of the P.E.O. Sisterhood, Alice Bird.

Chapter 2:
1866-1872

"Franc Rhodes (sic) was the girl with the far vision, and she was so progressive that she might have been set down in a college twenty-five years ahead of her time and not had to hasten her step to keep abreast. She was artistic and very beautiful, as her girlhood picture shows. No P.E.O. in the thirty thousand is one lap ahead of her today, and most of us are far in her wake."

Winona Reeves, The Story of P.E.O., 1919

History of Iowa Wesleyan

The "Historical Sketch and Alumni Record of Iowa Wesleyan College," published in 1917 states:

"In 1841, when Mt. Pleasant was but a hamlet of a few humble cottages, such men as I.I. Stewart, Peter Smith, E. Killpatrick, J.C. Hall, P.C. Tiffany, Samuel Nelson, Nelson Lathrop, John P. Grantham, and a score of others, 'whose names are as ointment poured forth,' in the memory of those days, were suggesting, counseling, planning, hoping, daring, and in 1842 meeting with the people en masse to discuss the relation of the hopes and future prosperity of the young territory to higher education. Of this labor of brain and heart Iowa Wesleyan was brought forth, first of all the educational institutions of her grade in Iowa, and first of all such institutions in the country on the west of the Mississippi."

As stated in the book, "The P.E.O. Founders' Scrapbook," with the promise of a free education for veteran soldiers, the end of the Civil War brings many men to Iowa Wesleyan. It is believed these soldiers could add breath and new life into the school, and to Mt. Pleasant, which suffers financial hardships during the War. The freshman class of 1865 names themselves the Lifebloods, to symbolize what they mean to the school and the community.

Entering Iowa Wesleyan in the fall of 1866, Franc did not enter Iowa Wesleyan with those freshman, but she completes her courses in three years; ending up with the Lifebloods graduating class of 1869.

It was only ten years before Franc enters Iowa Wesleyan, in 1856, when the first college-level graduate, Winfield Scott Mayne graduates from Iowa Wesleyan with a Bachelor of Arts degree.

Almost from the beginning, Iowa Wesleyan promotes opportunities for women in education. In 1859, Lucy Webster Killpatrick is the first woman to graduate. Interestingly, Franc's future father-in-law, Charles Elliott, is the President of the institution in 1859. Franc's future sister-in-law, Phebe Leech Elliott, graduates in 1860. She becomes a Professor of English Literature and Preceptors 1864-1865. She also serves as a member of the Board of Trustees at Iowa Wesleyan from 1870-1875.

In the spring of 1866, Arabella (Belle) Babb graduates with a law degree from Iowa Wesleyan and becomes the first woman to be admitted to the bar in the United States. In 1873, Bella's brother, Washington Irving Babb marries another founder of the P.E.O. Sisterhood, Alice Bird.

Dr. Charles Elliott, Franc's future father-in-law leaves his position as President of Iowa Wesleyan in September 1866 – just as Franc begins her studies. Rev. Charles Avery Holmes, A.M., D.D. becomes the new president. Rev. Holmes serves as president until January 1869; the same month as P.E.O. is founded. The Honorable James Harlan takes over and serves for one year until June of 1870. Because Harlan serves in the U.S. Senate at the same time; Rev. J. H. Hopkins, A.B., A.M., the Vice-President of Iowa Wesleyan, is acting President serving under Harlan.

Franc's Iowa Wesleyan and Post-Graduate Education

After three years of study, Franc is awarded a Bachelor of Science. Her chosen field of study is art. She is reported to have studied art, history, pedagogy and archeology. At the time, to earn a Master's degree, the requirement is to spend three years working within your field. Upon completion of the three years, a Master's of Science (A.M. degree) is awarded to Franc in 1872.

On 21 January 1869, Franc and six other women, Mary Allen, Alice Bird, Hattie Briggs, Alice Coffin, Suela Pearson and Ella Stewart begin the P.E.O. Sisterhood. In June of the same year, all but Suela and Ella graduate from Iowa Wesleyan. Twenty-four graduates are in the class of 1869; ten are women and fourteen are men. Half the women are the founders of P.E.O.

Census records indicate Franc is living with her parents in 1870. Family history of the Elliott family compiled by Franc's grandson and great-grandson, Dr. Frank Roads Elliott and Thomas Elliott, indicates Franc teaches in Mt. Pleasant

High School. Many women of the era become teachers, as it is one of the few occupations available to women. And, as teachers, the women often become disqualified to hold the position, if married.

Mary Allen, Alice Bird, Hattie Briggs, Alice Coffin and Franc were all awarded honorary Masters degrees in 1872. Mary marries in 1871, Alice in 1873, Hattie in 1873, and Franc in 1872. Suela Pearson, who graduates in with her Bachelor's Degree in 1871, marries in 1874. Alice Coffin and Ella Stewart never marry.

According to the 1917 "Iowa Wesleyan College Historical Sketch and Alumni Record," Franc goes on to do post graduate work at the University of Nebraska in Literature and History. She also studies at the Art Institute, Chicago. Additionally, the P.E.O. history book, "Out of the Heart," reports Franc "spends a winter of study at Rookwood Pottery in Cincinnati, Ohio; a summer in Europe, as well as participating in expanded studies at Columbia and Leland Stanford Universities."

Presumably, the study at Leland Stanford University is in 1918-1919. "Out of the Heart" mentions Franc stops on her way home to Chicago in Denver to attend the P.E.O. Convention held there 30 September to 3 October 1919. The book reports, Franc "had been in California the preceding year where she had worked on a thesis at the University of California, Berkeley."

"The Story of P.E.O.," written in 1923 by Winona Evans Reeves, provides more details about Franc's post-graduate studies at Leland Stanford: "While spending several months at Berkeley, she took a course in the university there, making a special study in the causes of World War. She has written much and used her influence in favor of constructive policy of arbitration as against the destruction and devastation of war." This same 1923 history states Franc (who is 70 years old) often "attends lectures at the University of Chicago with much regularity, sometimes taking a full course of lectures on a subject in which she is particularly interested."

Simon Charles Elliott

Simon is the ninth child born to Rev. Charles Elliott and his wife Phebe Leech Elliott. Prior to Simon's birth, Rev. Elliott immigrates to Ohio from Killybegs, Donegal, Ireland.

Rev. Elliott's father, John Elliott (1759-1809); grandfather to Simon, is a North Country (Ireland) farmer, a flax grower, whose family comes from Scotland. John Elliott's family is Protestant Scotch-Irish. Simon is the name also given of two of Rev. Elliott's brothers; one Simon, born in 1787, dies just three days prior his twenty-first birthday in 1808; the second Simon, is born in 1809. Simon's Uncle Simon later becomes a Methodist minister in Ohio.

According to the "Elliott Family History 1816-2003," authored by Earl S. Elliott, Rev. Charles is licensed to preach for the Irish Wesleyan Society in 1813. He converts to that religion in 1811 and receives ordination in the Methodist Church in 1813. Accounts of Rev. Charles Elliott's specific arrival date in America are conflicting; however, according to the Elliott family history, compiled by Dr. Frank Roads Elliott and Thomas Elliott, Charles' widowed mother and nine siblings immigrate with him. They arrive in Baltimore, Maryland and initially come across the Allegheny mountains in wagon trains, and on foot, to settle in Pennsylvania. Three other siblings to Rev. Elliott immigrate in 1819.

In 1814, the Elliott family settles in Ohio. Charles is admitted to the Ohio Annual Conference of the Methodist Episcopal Church in 1818.

From 1818 to 1822 Rev. Elliott travels the extensive church circuits; he's known as a circuit rider preacher. In this era, a circuit preacher is appointed to a geographic area and travels to multiple churches to preach.

In 1822, Rev. Elliott is appointed superintendent of the church mission at Upper Sandusky with the Wyandot Indians. Following that assignment, for the next five years, Rev. Elliott is presiding elder of the Ohio district. Several years later after his mission, Rev. Elliott writes a book based upon a journal he keeps during his time with the Wyandot Indians, "Missionary Reminiscences, Principally of the Wyandot Nation." An interesting side fact is Rev. Elliott's brother, John, builds a mission house for the Sandusky Indians.

Between the years 1827-1837, Charles is elected professor of languages at Madison College, Uniontown, Pennsylvania. By 1831, Rev. Elliott is stationed in Pittsburgh. While serving in Pittsburgh as presiding elder of that district, he is also chosen editor of the *Pittsburgh Conference Journal*.

The Elliott family history, compiled by Dr. Frank Roads Elliott and Thomas Elliott, discloses Phebe Leech Elliott, Simon's mother, is born in Mercer, Pennsylvania to his grandparents John Boyd Leech and Jane Morrison Leech. Although John Leech comes from Quaker and English ancestors, he and his wife Jane, marry outside the Quaker faith and are disowned. They join the Methodist Church. John donates land, as well as a parsonage, for the Old Salem Methodist Church in Mercer County. John is a surveyor by profession, however, he serves for 30 years as Justice of the Peace and at one time is an Auditor as well as a County Commissioner. Later in life, John is elected to represent Mercer County in the Pennsylvania Legislature; afterwards, he is elected to the Pennsylvania Senate. John also becomes a trustee of Allegheny College in Meadville, Pennsylvania.

John and Jane Leech's oldest son, David, is the founder in 1850 of Leechburg, located in Armstrong County, Pennsylvania.

The Elliott family history reveals Simon's mother, Phebe, meets Rev. Charles on the Leech farm, known as Leech's Corners, in Salem. Leech's Corners is a regular stop for Rev. Charles Elliott during his circuit travels. Salem Township is 30 miles east of Pittsburgh.

Phebe marries Rev. Charles Elliott 14 May 1822 in Salem, Mercer, Pennsylvania. Shortly after their wedding and for the next five years, Rev. Charles is assigned to the Wyandot Indians in Upper Sandusky. Upper Sandusky is 240 miles west of Pittsburgh. Phebe, Simon's mother, travels with Rev. Elliott during this mission.

Charles is appointed Professor of Languages for Madison College, Uniontown, Pennsylvania in 1827. The family remains there for four years. In 1831, he is stationed in Pittsburgh, Pennsylvania and by 1833 he becomes editor of the *Pittsburgh Conference Journal*.

In May of 1842, Rev. Elliott demonstrates his belief in education for women when he convenes an organizational meeting to begin Wesleyan Female College. By 1847, his daughter, Phebe, is found as a student at the school. Phebe's address is listed as Cincinnati; however, the family lives somewhere between the two cities, in or close to Muskingum County, Ohio, in 1843 when Simon is born.

On his volunteer enlistment application to the United States Army dated 9 May 1864, Simon Charles Elliott states he was born 23 December 1843 in Muskingum, Ohio. Although the application looks to read "Muskingham," no town with this name exists today. This could be the name of a long-gone location, or a clerical error as it is unknown if Simon personally completes the application or a clerk completes the application on his behalf.

Allegheny County, Pennsylvania, where Pittsburgh is located, borders on the eastern boundary of Muskingum County, Ohio.

Cincinnati is in Hamilton County, bordering county to Muskingum on the western border. It's close to 300 miles between Pittsburgh and Cincinnati.

It's not clear what specific year between 1831 and 1848 Rev. Elliott leaves Pittsburgh for Cincinnati.

According to the biography published in 1863 in "The New American Cyclopedia," after being the editor of *Pittsburgh Conference Journal* until 1848, Rev. Elliott becomes editor of the *Western Christian Advocate* in Cincinnati, a post he holds for many years.

Simon's sister, Phebe, continues to be on the Wesleyan Female College school rooster during the terms 1848-1849, 1852-1853, and 1854-1855. Another of Simon and Phebe's siblings, Fannie, is also listed as a student at the school during the 1854-1855 term.

By July of 1850, when Simon is age 6, the 1850 US Federal Census depicts Rev. Elliott, Simon and the Elliott family living in Xenia, Green County, Ohio. Xenia is 100 miles southwest of Upper Sandusky.

In an interesting historical side note, under the U.S. Indian Removal policy, the Wyandots are made to give up their claims to their reservation in Upper Sandusky in 1842 (20 years after Rev. Elliott's assignment with them). This treaty requires the Wyandot Indians to sell their land at a price under fair market value. They leave for Kansas and move to what is now Wyandotte County, Kansas.

It is 26 November 1857 when Rev. Charles Elliott, D.D. LL. D. is elected President of Iowa Wesleyan. Rev. Elliott serves two terms as President. His first term is 26 November 1857 to 22 June 1861. His second term is from 23 June 1863 to 26 September 1866. During Rev. Elliott's first term, he again demonstrates his interest in education for women, by assuring the first woman, Lucy Killpatrick, graduates from Iowa Wesleyan with the first Baccalaureate degree granted a woman from a co-educational institution.

We learn within the book, "Historical Sketch and Alumni Record of Iowa Wesleyan College," published in 1917, during the time of the Civil War, and in the interim between his two Presidencies, Dr. Elliott is editor of the *Central Christian Advocate*, St. Louis. He is cited as being "bold, daring, aggressive, and sometimes defiant in the Union cause. He earned for himself the name of War Editor."

Dr. Elliott's term as President is one of struggles to find funds for the school operations, the mortgage payment on Old Main and the necessary building repairs. Because the Civil War causes a decline in student enrollments, President Elliott combines professorships to enable the school to survive. It isn't until 1865, when the first of the founders begin at the college, that a new influx of students gives new life to the college.

By the time of his death in 1869, it's been expressed Rev. Elliott, due to his remarkable propensity for languages, had grasp of nine languages.

Within the Elliott family history compiled by Rev. Charles Elliott's great-grandson and great-great-grandson, Dr. Frank Roads Elliott and Thomas Elliott, we read, "His speech betrayed his nationality, and his Irish brogue was rather difficult to understand. Charles was so absent-minded that when out on his preaching tours he was apt to gather into his saddle bags things that did not belong to him, and leave his own behind. His daughter once found in the miscellaneous assortment a sunbonnet and a child's gingham dress. In the midst of a scholarly address at the commencement of the Miami Medical College he had occasion to use a handkerchief. He thrust his hand into his pocket and drew out an enormous yellow bandanna. He looked at it fondly for a moment, then shook his head regretfully and returned it. Next, he drew out of the opposite pocket a clean linen handkerchief neatly folded. Shaking his head approvingly he proceeds to use it. The audience was convulsed at this pantomimic betrayal of feminine home instructions.

Once preaching in Wesley Chapel he became so impassioned that with a violent gesture he swept his manuscript off the pulpit. He paused and said laconically, 'Ah, I've lose me nuts,' and proceeded without their aid. He invariably spoke of the Pope as the 'Pup in Run.' It was his brogue, however, he meant no disrespect to His Holiness."

In the 1860 U.S. Federal Census, at the age of 16, Simon is listed as living with his parents in Mt. Pleasant, Henry County, Iowa.

The Civil War begins in 1861 and as mentioned previously, in May of 1864 Simon volunteers for 100 days of service. During the height of the Civil War it becomes increasingly difficult to obtain troops for the Union Army. The troops that enlist in this program are to perform routine duties, which will allow veteran soldiers to go to the front combat lines in an all-out effort to end the war. Once enlisted, these men receive short training and are ready for service within sixteen days.

Simon is a member of Company A of the 45th Iowa Volunteer Infantry Regiment; one among many troops that are raised during the summer of 1864. This Regiment, commanded by Alvah H. Bereman, organizes at Keokuk, Iowa. The Regiment musters in on 25 May 1864 and musters out on 15 September 1864. As previously mentioned, this Regiment moves to St. Louis, then to Memphis and Moscow, Tennessee. The men are assigned to guarding strategic points on the Memphis and Charleston Railroad until they muster out in September.

Another member of this Regiment, who mustered in and out on the same days as Simon, is William Rose Pearson, brother to P.E.O. founder Suela Pearson.

According to Simon's military records, he joins duty as a Private on 18 May 1864 in Birmingham, Iowa by enlisting within the First Congressional District of Iowa. There is a note on his application indicating his residence is Vernon; 20 miles south of Birmingham. Vernon is also located 40 miles southwest of Mt. Pleasant.

An additional notation is found indicating Simon is left in a hospital in a convalescent camp near Memphis from 25 May – just seven days after he joined duty - until 26 June.

Military records describe Simon as being 5 feet 8 1/2 inches tall, with light complexion, sandy hair and blue eyes.

Stella Clap, in "Out of the Heart," tells us Simon is often mentioned as an escort of Franc's during her college years; as well as post-college years, and prior to their marriage. Interestingly, "Out of the Heart" also mentions there is no record recorded for Simon graduating from Iowa Wesleyan. Indeed, Simon is not found listed as a graduate of Iowa Wesleyan in the book, "Iowa Wesleyan College - Its History and Its Alumni 1842-1917." However, "Out of the Heart" author Stella Clap, speculates Simon may have been a student during the years his father, Rev. Charles Elliott was President.

Within his military pension application, Simon states he lives in Lincoln, Nebraska starting in 1869. He presumably leaves Mt. Pleasant, after his father's death (January 1869) and goes to the Lincoln area as a pioneer to begin his own career.

Being created in 1854, Nebraska becomes a territory. In 1867, Nebraska is the 37th state to be admitted to the Union. The city of Lincoln is created in 1867 and becomes the capital city of Nebraska two years prior to when Simon goes to seek his fortune.

The "History of Nebraska" found at Wikipedia states during the 1870's and 1880's Civil War veterans (such as Simon) and immigrants come "by the thousands" to Nebraska.

The "Historical Sketches of the University of Nebraska," published within the book, "Semi-Centennial Anniversary Book-The University of Nebraska 1869-1919," reminds readers when we think of early pioneers to Nebraska, "We are likely to forget that they were a special breed of men, especially rich in ambitions and ideals, richer in these, it may well be, than many of us who are their descendants." The reflection continues; "They surrendered many things when they came to these plains. Ties of kinship, of friendship, and endearing association bound them to older localities. It is only men of strong individuality who break such bonds, and face undaunted the self-denials and privations of frontier life."

One compelling reason Simon relocates to Lincoln may be his sister, Phebe. Historical accounts written by historian Jim McKee and published in the *Lincoln Journal Star* recount: "Phoebe (sic) Elliott, for whom Elliott School was later named, taught the first school in a log cabin near Saltillo, a village near the southeast corner of Wilderness Park." Within a separate article referring to Phebe, Mr. McKee writes: "Simon

Bernadom, one of Lincoln's first settlers and the area's first fur buyer, reported the 'first school in the county was one and one-half miles north of the town of Roca.' The first school building was a log cabin on a sand hill and simply known as Sandhill School. The first, and possibly the only, teacher was Miss Phoebe (sic) L. Elliott."

It is estimated Phebe teaches in this school 1864-1865. Phebe may have encouraged Simon to move to Lincoln because of the opportunities to be found. Indeed, in a 1920 letter written to friends in Nebraska and published in the *Sunday State Journal*, Phebe mentions she is a resident of Lincoln "before the railroad arrived." The first railroad, the Burlington and Missouri River Railroad, arrives in Lincoln in July 1870.

Simon is listed in the 1870 United States Census as living in a hotel in Lincoln. He indicates his occupation is "Drug Merchant."

However, we find his sister, Phebe L. Elliott, living in 1870 in Mt. Pleasant with their mother, Phebe Leach Elliott. Perhaps Simon's sister feels the need to move back to Iowa after her and Simon's father's death in January of 1869.

Simon and Franc marry on 6 June 1872. The ceremony is conducted by Rev. John Haynes, a member of the Iowa Conference of the Methodist Episcopal Church.

The following, a sworn statement by Simon's sister, Phebe, provided after Simon's death, attests to the marriage of Simon and Franc. This document, dated 1915, states: "She (Phebe) has known him (Simon) personally since the day of his birth and been intimate with him and his family and has had personal knowledge of his family relations. He was married to Miss Franc Rodes (sic) on the 7th (sic) of June 1872. He had never been married to any other person prior to that time. She knew Miss Rodes (sic) for several years prior to her said marriage to Simon C. Elliott and she had never been married to anyone else prior to that time. They were never divorced or separated but lived together up to the time of Simon C. Elliott's death, as stated. That the said Franc R. Elliott, his widow, has not remarried since his death."

Chapter 3: 1872-1893

"Franc Roads Elliott married Simon Elliott, whose father was the learned Dr. Elliott, at one-time president of Iowa Wesleyan. When she called on her return visits, I can remember how my mother was refreshed by her delightful conversation on art and current topics, for she was a brilliant woman, and she brought ideas from the outside world."

> Quote from Clara Bird Knopp (1870-1953),
> the daughter of Hiram Thornton Bird and
> Mary Florence McLeran and niece to Alice Bird Babb

Life in Nebraska for Franc 1872-1893

The year 1869, when Simon begins living in Lincoln, is transformational for him, for he not only leaves Mt. Pleasant, but his father, Rev. Charles Elliott and his sister, Fanny Blaine Elliott, both die during the year. Simon's father, Charles dies in January and his sister, Fanny in March.

In 1872, the newlyweds make their home in Lincoln, Nebraska, 350 miles from Mt. Pleasant, Iowa. By then, Nebraska has only been a state for five years. "Out of the Heart" states, "eventually, they (Simon and Frank) built a gabled cottage on 14th Street just south of M, where they lived for many years."

An article in local newspaper, *The Lincoln Star*, dated 12 August 1924, comments, "The first classes in art and ceramics and the first firing kiln for china in Lincoln were Mrs. Elliott's. She came to Lincoln as a bride in 1870 (sic) and made her house on the southwest corner of Fourteenth and M Streets."

Not long after Franc and Simon marry, Franc gives birth to their first child, Charles Addison Elliott. Presumably named for both of his grandfathers, Charles Elliott and Addison Roads, Charles is born in Lincoln on 6 March 1873.

Lincoln is also where Stella May Elliott, Franc and Simon's second child, their daughter, is born 31 October 1876.

Franc begins teaching art in Lincoln 1876-1877.

The 1880 Nebraska state and the 1880 United States federal censuses, lists the household members Simon, Franc, Charles and Stella living on M Street. Living with the family is Anyalina Tebrink, who is serving the family as a cook.

During the 1880's, Simon is a china store merchant. Within the book "Out of the Heart," we discover the store is a Queen's Ware Store; a specific brand of china.

According to Merriam-Webster's dictionary, Queen's Ware is defined as "a specific type of dinnerware that was custom designed for one of England's Queens. It is typified by an embossed ivy leaf or similar border around the pieces. While piece shapes, colors and borders vary slightly, through the years, it has maintained its standard style." Wedgwood china is an example of Queen's Ware china.

The Elliott's store is known as "S.C. Elliott's Crockery Store" and occasionally as "S.C. Elliott's China Hall." The earliest reference found in the Lincoln newspaper, *The Nebraska State Journal*, to the store is October 1876. Initially located at the corner of 11th and O Street, the store is later situated within a building known as the Elliott block, at 1212 O Street in Lincoln. There are offices within the building over the store occupied by variety of professionals, including lawyers and judges.

Franc expands her interest in art and becomes proficient in the art of china painting. Franc's art studio is also referenced as being over the store. From the family history compiled by Dr. Frank Roads Elliott and Thomas Elliott, we understand beginning 1883-1884 Franc runs an artist studio next to S.C. Elliott's china store where she "mastered china painting and gave lessons in drawing and painting."

A contemporary of Franc, Maria Longwoth Nicholas Storer, initiates Rookwood Pottery in 1880 in Cincinnati. At the time, Rookware pottery is acknowledged as being a "popular American art pottery, designed to be at least as useful as it is decorative."

Franc studies china painting at Rookwood. Conceivably, she is studying at Rookwood when Clara Chipman Newton works at Rockwood as a china decorator during the first decade of the institute's history. Clara has a similar life path to Franc. According to a history of Rookwood, Clara is celebrated as a "champion of new media and what she called 'women's work,' by pursuing her activism through a variety of arts-and-crafts organizations." Clara is also a founding member of the Cincinnati Woman's Club.

Franc and Simon are mentioned in a 9 December 1882 *Omaha Daily Bee* newspaper article as attending the silver wedding anniversary party of Dr. and Mrs. Mathewson. The party attracts seventy-five guests. It is noted the party is not being largely attended. The report remarks it's likely because the party is held at the insane asylum, located about three miles from town, and the weather was cold.

In June of 1884, an article appearing in the *Nebraska State Journal* confirms Franc is teaching art classes in Lincoln 1875-1876:

"Mrs. Elliott's Art Reception - A Fine Exhibition of the Work of Lincoln Artists

Mrs. S.C. Elliott has been teaching painting in Lincoln for eight or nine years, and the constant increase in the number of her pupils and the excellence of her work are the best recommendation that can be given of her work. Last year she gave an exhibition of the work of her classes at Fawell's book store, but last night's reception was the first exhibition which she has given at the studio. A June exhibition will be a regular feature hereafter.

The rooms of the studio presented a beautiful appearance last evening. The walls and table were covered with works of art in various forms, landscape, fruit, flower and face paintings, fire screens, decorated mirrors and other articles, panels, plaques, china work, and other works of art too numerous to mention. There were too many to permit of noticing each one, and we will have to content ourselves with making mention of a few of the most remarkable features.

Much attention was attracted by the work in china. Some of this work displayed exquisite taste and all was excellent. Mrs. S.S. Brock deserves especial mention in this connection. The berry and ice cream sets of her work on exhibition were simply exquisite and were the subject of many enthusiastic expressions of admiration. Misses Tote McMurtry and Lizzie Weston had some after dinner coffee sets which showed some very skillful work, and a tea set and berry set decorated by Mrs. Elliott could not be surpassed anywhere. An interesting feature in the execution of this work is the firing after the painting is done by which the designs are set. Until this year all work had to be sent away to be fired and it was thought that it could not be done here. Mrs. Elliott has demonstrated that it can, however, and now does all this work in her own kiln.

Among the paintings worthy of notice we may mention two faces by Mrs. S.S. Brock, which showed several points of artistic excellence. A figure of Cupid on a satin panel, painted by Mrs. Elliott, was a dainty little bit of work that was much admired. A single peacock feather upon bolting cloth, under which was placed white silk, was exhibited by Mrs. Ed Baum. The bolting cloth as a ground for the work lent a peculiar delicacy to it that added greatly to the effect. A fire screen ornamented with peonies by Mrs. Walter Hargreaves, and another by Mrs. W.W. Holmes; two panels of wild flowers, in plush frames, from the brush of Mrs. Elliott: a fire screen, painted on plush, by Miss Lena Marshall, and a landscape by Mrs. Elliott, are among the works which should not pass unnoticed.

Some vases made by Mrs. Elliott while in Chicago, and a pitcher and several tea cups and saucers made by Mrs. Brock, also while in Chicago, were much admired.

The exhibition, on the whole, was one which reflected credit, both on the classes and on Mrs. Elliott as instructor. It was a decided success, and was the source of much pleasure to the lovers of art who attended. Mrs. Elliott request us to extend to all interested in art an invitation to call at any time tomorrow afternoon, or in the evening, at the same hours as were observed last evening, from 8 to 11.

Mrs. Elliott had not intended to teach this summer, but has changed her mind, and will begin a summer term next week."

In addition, during 1884 Franc is appointed as a State Superintendent to represent Nebraska at the New Orleans Cotton Centennial Exposition; often referred to as the 1884 World's Fair. The Exposition is established to celebrate the hundredth anniversary of the first export of cotton from the United States in 1784. According to the "Story of P.E.O." written by Winona Evans Reeves in 1923, Franc is the first women commissioner named in any world's exposition.

Early in September, a plea to the "Ladies of Omaha and Douglas County" is published in the *Omaha Daily Bee*:

"Director-General Burke, of the World's Industrial and Cotton Centennial Exposition, to be held in New Orleans this coming winter, says that 'doubtless the national exposition of woman's work will be one of the most important and interesting exhibitions of that wonderfully magnificent scheme.' The woman can respond by sending something of the best of her handiwork. Loyalty to your state demands this of you, to be well represented, and show the world that even we of the prairies can appreciate the beautiful as well as the useful. At a meeting held in Lincoln, which organized the Nebraska State association for the exhibition of woman's work at the New Orleans Worlds exposition, I was appointed state superintendent of fine arts. I now call upon every lady in the state who is interested in art work of any kind - painting in oil, China color, water color, pastel, crayon and charcoal drawing, modeling, carving in wood, to send samples of your skill to this exhibition. Lincoln and Omaha have been chosen as general receiving points to which exhibits should be sent, where great care will be exercised in packing and shipping to New Orleans free of all charges. These exhibits must be shipped from collecting points by Nov 15. For further information address Mrs. S.C. Elliott, State Superintendent of Fine Arts for World's Exposition, 1212 O Street, Lincoln, Nebraska."

In December, Franc again reaches out to the women of Nebraska through newspaper articles such as this one published 18 December 1884 in the *McCook Weekly Tribune*.

"To Nebraska Women. - It is desirous that Nebraska women's work be well represented at this New Orleans World's Exposition. Through the efforts of some of our enterprising ladies we have a very fair exhibit - considering the time given for collecting - consisting mainly of knitting, needle and decorative work, besides a good culinary exhibit, but we are deficient in lines of work in which I am sure many of our Nebraska women are proficient, and by which they are enabled to support themselves. Desirous of obtaining the articles which represent such occupations, I make this appeal to Nebraska women who are interested in following lines of work, and ask that models or samples be sent to my address: Inventions, domestic or other, originated by women; a copy of every book published or newspaper edited by women; editorials, poems or literary articles written by women; type-writing, stenographic work, penmanship, business cards; samples of silk, wool, flax, or cotton grown by women; samples of same spun or woven; samples of grain grown by women.

Let Nebraska women interest themselves in these things, thus aiding toward making the Nebraska woman's work a feature of the woman's department as our state exhibit is of the states display. Send by registered mail or express to my address, Mrs. S.C. Elliott, Commissioner for Neb. Woman's Work, New Orleans, La."

To highlight Woman's Work, according to Robert W. Furnas's final report of the event, the Nebraska exhibit also contains a document on education, representations of the Benevolent and Humane Department work within the state, industrial arts (carpets, tapestries, laces, knitting, quilting, crochet work) and samples from the culinary department, of "elaborately decorated and artistic appearance."

Unfortunately, the Exposition is in debt and opens two weeks late on 16 Dec 1884. It remains open until 31 May 1885. Some of the exhibits aren't fully completed until March of 1885. The "New Orleans Centennial Exposition Stereoscopic Views" reports a total of 1,158,840 visitors attend. However, that number is far below the projected estimate of 4 million. The Exposition closes 2 June 1885 with a debt of nearly half-million dollars.

On 11 March 1885, Nebraska Day is celebrated at the Exposition. The summary Report of Robert W. Furnas, Commissioner relates:

"..the *Times-Democrat*, the leading New Orleans daily, said: The Nebraska reception was pronounced by all who were so fortunate as to be present last Wednesday, at the government building of the Exposition, to be the most elegant and recherche affair of the kind that has been attempted by any of the states represented, and every way in keeping with the beautiful exhibit that has excited unbounded admiration of all beholders, for the requisite taste displayed in the decoration and beautiful designs executed with such artistic taste in the grains and grasses of this state.

Well may the representatives of Nebraska be proud of not only their state, but the successful management of this gala day reception. Nebraska's head-quarters are as handsome as a lady's boudoir, and the walls are decorated with bright colored wall-paper, with fringe made of red and yellow corn. It is a matter of continued astonishment how anything so homely in itself, say the corn cob and grains of corn, can so deftly be made to serve the purpose of beautifying wall panels and posts."

On 16 May 1885, Robert W. Furnas, United States Commissioner for Nebraska to the New Orleans writes a letter to Franc. A copy of the letter is found within the 1885 "Report of Robt. W. Furnas, United States Commissioner for Nebraska at the World's Industrial and Cotton Centennial New Orleans." As a side point of interest, Robert W. Furnas served as the second Governor of Nebraska 1873-1875.

"Mrs. S.C. Elliott,

Dear Madam: Fully appreciating as I do, and have from the commencement of our work, your valuable assistance in presenting the Nebraska exhibit at New Orleans, I desire to acknowledge your services in a more fitting, substantial, and enduring manner than mere expression of thanks, feeling well assured that in so doing I but voice the sentiments of every Nebraskan, as well as all others who witnessed the part you have taken, and the work you have performed. To this end I tender you the accompanying gold medal, in design indicating Wisdom, Industry, Art, and Music. I trust this souvenir will serve to remind you, and even your 'children's children' that you have fairly won the plaudit, 'Well done, thou good and faithful one.'

In addition, accept, please, my thanks, with best wishes for your future happiness and usefulness,

Very truly yours, Robt. W. Furnas, U.S. Com for Nebraska"

Throughout the commissioner's Report, reference to Franc is found as "the lady Commissioner of Nebraska." Also noted in the report is Franc's sister-in-law, Phebe L. Elliott, who assists Franc with efforts in the Woman's Work department, and in placing materials in the educational exhibit.

"The P.E.O. in Illinois: A History," published in 1953, credits this Exposition as the place where Franc "came into association with intellectuals of every sort. The women commissioners with many others, came together to hear Julia Ward Howe, Elizabeth Cady Stanton, Susan B. Anthony, Lucy Stone, Francis Willard and the poet Whittier. Two favorite themes were the franchise of women and the abolishment of war."

One of the many organizations in which Franc participates is the Women's Christian Association (WCA) in Lincoln.

A brief overview of the Lincoln WCA group was given to *The Nebraska State Journal* by its president, Mrs. J. I. Underwood, in October 1893. In that interview, she states the

WCA was organized in 1886 as one of the first organizations in Nebraska to "help self-supporting women and young women, temporally, morally, mentally and religiously." Mrs. Underwood reports between 1886 and 1893 the Lincoln WCA accomplishes: "establishing reading rooms in downtown Lincoln offering working women a suitable, comfortable place to spend the noon hour while eating their lunches; conducting bible classes and gospel services for working women; opening a boarding home for self-supporting women; establishing an employment bureau for women; offering medical advice and treatment at a WCA dispensary; offering transient homes – a cheap place where women can remain while seeking work or friends; establishing 'Stranger's Friend,' which includes placing cards at railway stations and providing a motherly person to visit the trains daily and rendering aid to girls who come as strangers into the city; visiting the sick and poor to relieve their distress in many kindly ways; establishing a Tobitha hospital committee, which contributes donations and volunteers for work for the hospital." They also "support a bed for any women who might be in need of a hospital bed; conduct devotional meetings each month and a prayer meeting each week for young women."

An article published in the *Omaha Daily*, 17 October 1891, reports Franc is one of the two delegates elected to represent the International Women's Christian Association at the November 1891 World's Women's Christian Temperance union convention in Boston.

The 1917 "Iowa Wesleyan College – Its History and Its Alumni 1842-1917," reflects that while living in Lincoln, Nebraska in 1887, Franc is "prominent in the first movement of looking toward admission of women to general conference" of the Methodist Episcopal Church. Franc maintains her ties to the Methodist Episcopal Church after her marriage to Simon; whose father had been a Reverend in the Methodist Episcopal Church.

Indeed, within the "History of Nebraska Methodism, the First Half-Century 1854-1904," is found a lengthy tribute to Franc and her sister-in-law, Phebe. This tribute acknowledges the role Franc and Phebe play in advancing the role of women in the church, by their advocating the admission to women to the Methodist General Conference in the spring of 1887.

This history recounts the origins of the concept of the movement to admit women to the Conference occurs at St. Paul's Church in Lincoln that spring: "The two women whose fertile brains first conceived the thought, and broached the subject to the other ladies of the Church on the occasion of the dedication of the dining-room of the Church, were Miss Phebe Elliott and Mrs. Franc R. Elliott. Both these elect ladies, as might be readily supposed, were of superior intelligence and force of character."

According to church history found at the United Methodist Church website, it is Frances Willard (1838-1898) who "brought the involvement of women in and through the Methodist Church very much into the foreground." Frances Willard and 'five other women' are elected to serve as delegates to the 1888 General Conference in New York. Could Franc and Phebe be two of the "five other women?"

Within the "History of Nebraska Methodism" account, Phebe credits her "father's teachings of absolute equality of the sexes in all that relates to mind, morals, and religion, and the rights growing out of this," as the basis for her beliefs. The commentary also reports Phebe made her home with her sister-in-law, Franc.

Within the story, "The P.E.O. in Illinois: A History," is found another reference to Franc's efforts, "for some eighteen years she worked to secure for women the right of a seat and vote in the General Conference of the Methodist Episcopal church. That accomplishment later brought certain privileges to women of other denominations."

Elsewhere in Franc's family, in 1888, Addison Roads, Franc's father is elected County Treasurer for two terms in Henry County, Iowa. And, on 28 July 1890, a new post office is established in McClureville, Iowa. This post office is named for Franc's first cousin, George D. McClure, postmaster for McClureville. McClureville is in the southeast quarter of the southwest quarter of Section 32 in Jefferson township, Iowa. Today, the town no longer exists.

On 5 Oct 1889, the following is published in the *Capital City Courier* of Lincoln, Nebraska:

"Mrs. S.C. Elliott, one of the enthusiastic graduates of the CLSC, is not only pursuing a post-graduate course in Chautauqua study, but has taken up a literary course in the State university. She has company in the latter in the person of Miss Elliott, and their industry is greatly admired."

Franc's daughter, Stella, was thirteen in 1889, thus the Miss Elliott referenced could be her sister-in-law, Miss Phebe Elliott. Indeed, in October 1888, an announcement of the first meeting of The Capital CLSC (Chautauqua Literary and

Scientific Circle) appears in the *Nebraska State Journal*. The article highlights the program will include a paper on the Chautauqua idea, presented by Miss Phebe Elliott. The motivation for the name "The Capital CLSC" is apt to be due to Lincoln being the capital of Nebraska.

The Chautauqua Institution website (www.chq.org) describes its history: Chautauqua Lake Sunday School Assembly, now known as Chautauqua Institution, was founded in 1874 by Lewis Miller and John Heyl Vincent "as an educational experiment in out-of-school, vacation learning. It was successful and broadened almost immediately beyond courses for Sunday school teachers to include academic subjects, music, art and physical education."

Lewis Miller is a businessman and philanthropist credited as inventor of the first combine with the blade "efficiently in front of the driver, to the side of the horse." Mina Miller, daughter to Lewis, marries Thomas Alva Edison in 1886.

His partner, John Heyl Vincent, is a bishop of the Methodist Episcopal Church. Beginning in 1878, he becomes Chancellor of Chautauqua Institution.

The program Franc attends held at the same location, is the Chautauqua Literary and Scientific Circle (CLSC) which starts in 1878 "to provide those who could not afford the time or money to attend college the opportunity of acquiring the skills and essential knowledge of a College education. The four-year, correspondence course was one of the first attempts at distance learning."

The idea behind the program is to "show people how best to use their leisure time and avoid the growing availability of idle past times, such as drinking, gambling, dancing and theater-going, that posed a threat both to good morals and to good health....At the end of their four years of study, students were invited to come to Chautauqua to receive their certificates in a ceremony, which is still held today during the first week of August."

The program is so successful it becomes known as the "Chautauqua Movement." This history continues, "By 1880 the Chautauqua platform had established itself as a national forum for open discussion of public issues, international relations, literature and science. Among those who benefited most from the CLSC program were women, teachers, and those living in remote rural areas."

Two more references to Franc's visits to Chautauqua, New York occur in the Lincoln newspaper, *The Courier*; 30 August 1890 which states: "Mrs. S.C. Elliott and daughter Stella have returned from an extended visit at Chautauqua;" and, on 2 September 1899 within the article reporting the wedding of Franc's daughter, Stella Elliott, and James Canfield on 18 August 1899.

Upon occasion, small news items about Franc and Simon appear in the local newspapers, such as the item published 21 May 1892, in which the *Capital City Courier* reports "Mr. and Mrs. S.C. Elliott returned Thursday from Florida."

Within a December 1897 letter from a Cleve L. Green to the editor of *The Courier*, Franc is reported as being a member of the "pioneer Shakespere (sic) club." This women's club is organized a year or two prior to any other official women's club. Because the Lincoln Woman's Club begins about 1894, it's assumed this Shakespeare club is an organization Franc participates in during the time frame of 1892-1893.

The book "The Story of P.E.O.," published in 1923, reports Franc "was the first instructor of art in the Nebraska State University-where her two children were educated." The University of Nebraska, however, is unable to substantiate specific dates when Franc may have taught any classes.

The United States economy in 1893 takes several hits leading to the "Panic of 1893." In February, the Philadelphia and Reading Railroad fails. During May, the National Cordage Company collapses. This same company experiences an initial public offering of five million dollars at the beginning of the 1890s. During the first months of 1893, six hundred banks fail. In April, the United States Treasury's gold reserves fall below $100 million, which sets off a financial panic. By the end of 1893, four thousand banks fold. It's estimated fourteen thousand businesses also meet with disaster.

Nebraska State Historical Society relates a picture of life in Nebraska during this era:

"Nebraska in the early 1890's suffered from protracted drought, and farm prices fell to new lows. Conditions were so unfavorable that immigration, which had more than doubled the state's population in the 1880's almost ceased. Nebraska's population increased by seven thousand persons between 1890 and 1900. Some became so discouraged that they sold or gave up their property and left the state.

Charles H. Morrill, a prominent farmer, businessman, and banker for whom Morrill County, Nebraska was named, both witnessed and experienced these conditions in Nebraska. In his autobiographical 'The Morrills and Reminiscences,' published in 1918, he recalls:

'In the year 1893 crops in Nebraska were almost totally destroyed by drought and hot winds. Then came the panic and financial stress, which paralyzed business. In 1894 Nebraska was doomed to have another crop failure. Farmers were obliged to ship in grain and even hay to feed their stock; many sacrificed their livestock by selling at very low prices. Some farmers shot their stock hogs to prevent their starving. Financial conditions grew worse and the entire state was almost in the grip of actual famine.

Values were greatly reduced, merchants and banks failed. In Lincoln, all banks with the exception of three went out of business or failed. Farmers could not pay interest on their mortgages; land could not be sold at any price; foreclosure of mortgages was the general order....In the central and western sections of the state the price of land fell to almost nothing. In Custer County, a very large acreage went into the ownership of eastern real estate and loan companies. These lands were mortgaged for five hundred to seven hundred dollars on each one hundred and sixty acres. One eastern loan company offered to sell me forty quarter sections at two hundred dollars each.

The crop for 1895 was almost a failure. The result was that all confidence in Nebraska real estate was gone...Good farm lands in Polk and other eastern counties sold as low as twenty-five hundred dollars for one hundred and sixty acres. Many of these farms had improvements thereon valued at fifteen hundred to two thousand dollars. No one desired to purchase while almost everyone wished to sell.

Urban areas didn't escape the effects of the drought and depression. *Figaro*, an Omaha weekly, on December 2, 1893, noted that at the time of the recent Thanksgiving holiday, there were 'two thousand people in Omaha homeless and absolutely without means of support.' The newspaper urged its readers to 'find at least one of these unfortunates a place to sleep and enough to eat to sustain life without actual misery.'

The financial depression reached its summit in the period 1894-96 but continued into the year 1897. By 1898 there were signs that better times were returning. Those who managed to hold on during the hard times were rewarded by returning prosperity in the early years of the twentieth century."

According to the family history compiled by Dr. Frank Roads Elliott and Thomas Elliott, Franc and Simon lose everything in 1893. Referring to Franc, they write, "she was 41 and 20 years out of college. She started right in with grim determination by opening and kept a big rooming house in Chicago during the World's Fair."

The World's Fair referenced by Mr. Elliott is the World's Columbian Exposition, also known as the Chicago Worlds' Fair. The Fair is held to acknowledge the 400th anniversary of Christopher Columbus's arrival in the Americas.

Elliott's Land Transactions

Between the years of 1879 and 1937, the Lincoln newspapers report a variety of real estate transactions pertaining to the building where Simon's business is located. In 1879, a newspaper listing for real estate transactions indicates Simon, acting as attorney-in-fact for Phebe Elliott, deeds partial pieces of lots 10 and 11, block 53 to a CW and WW Marsh. It is unknown if the Phebe Elliott mentioned is Simon's mother or his sister.

On 27 September 1883, a real estate transfer notice appears in the Nebraska State Journal reflecting the transfer of "7 1/2 feet off east side lot 11, also the west 1/2, lot 10, block 53, Lincoln" from Simon and Phebe, executor and executrix, to CW and WM Marsh. This notice, listing Simon and Phebe his sister as estate executors, would lend credibility to the fact that Simon and Phebe's mother, Phebe Elliott (1803-1882) was an owner of property in Lincoln. Indeed, Phebe Leech Elliott's will, written in October of 1881, 11 months before her death, alludes to the fact she owns several pieces of property. According to directions found in her will, Phebe Leech Elliott owns a Mt. Pleasant, Iowa house, "which is to be given to her daughter, Phebe, and all other property which is to be liquidated as necessary to fulfill her wishes of various cash inheritances for her children and grandchildren" as designated in her will.

By following the paper trail, it appears Simon initially purchases lots where the building is located as the above referenced 1879, either with or on behalf of his sister or mother. Through the years a few more transactions are made, including the sale of the lots in 1883 which list both Simon and his sister Phebe as executors of their mother's estate.

Additionally, Franc, together with Simon's sister, Phebe, purchase lots in the same location in May 1887.

The last recorded transaction reported in the Lincoln newspaper is on 15 Sept 1937, when Stella Elliott Canfield and her husband James Canfield, Franc and Simon's daughter and son-in-law, are reported as selling the building which housed Simon's store.

Simon C. Elliott and His Store

In addition to owning the S.C. Elliott store, Simon becomes involved within the Lincoln community. He runs for the office of City Treasurer in 1878, but loses his bid to win.

During the 1880's Simon continues to grow, promote and manage the crockery/china store.

Between the years of 1876 and 1890 multiple advertisements are placed by Elliott's in the local Lincoln newspapers. Some are one-line ads such as one published 17 Dec 1881, stating "Holiday Goods at Elliotts." Some are larger sized ads, such as one published 30 June 1887, advertising, "The Alaska Dry Air Refrigerators, for sale by S.C. Elliott, Crockery, China, Glassware, Rochester Lamps, and Lamp Goods."

Simon is elected Reporter of the Knights of Honor organization in December 1881.

On 14 September 1886, *The Nebraska State Journal* of Lincoln, Nebraska carries the following story:

"A Little Twister Tears Down Several Walls and Plays Havoc Generally

The East Wall of the Baldwin Block Caves in the Roof of the Adjoining Store - a Large Stock of China Goods Destroyed - Heavy Damage to a Fifteen Street Building - A Destructive Whirlwind

The most violent and destructive wind storm of the season visited this city at 3:45 yesterday afternoon, causing considerable damage. The most appalling indication of its presence is the generally wrecked condition of the Baldwin Bros. Building now in course of construction near the corner of Twelfth and O streets. During the extremely heavy rain which accompanied the wind a terrific crash in that vicinity startled people for several blocks around.

Shortly before the catastrophe to the Baldwin building the clerks in the employ of S.C. Elliott, the porcelain dealer next door - east, had rushed to the front doors with a view to closing same to shut out the wind. Mr. Elliott, who was employed in the office in the rear part of the store, also arose and began securing the back door. Hardly had these operations commenced within a thundering crash came, filling the store with the debris of the roof, which came roaring down upon several counters loaded with china goods and crockery of every description. The rear part of the Elliott store is only one story in height and when a section of the wall of the Baldwin building fell upon the roof its weight carried everything before it. The scene in the store immediately after the catastrophe was interesting, to say the least. A section of the roof thirty feet in length and extending to both walls lay in an almost inextricable mass on the floor. Buried beneath the debris of rafters, joists, tin and rafters lay four counters, upon which had been displayed elegant stocks of colored and decorated china ware, hanging lamps, and bric-a-brac. The shelves lining the wall were crushed with their contents to the floor. On all sides lay in profusion splintered glass, the whole forming a picture never before seen in this city.

Mr. S.C. Elliott, who was seen by a reporter for THE JOURNAL a few moments after the accident, stated in reference to the loss sustained by him that he could at the time form no proper estimate. He felt thankful, he said, that no one was injured. A few moments before he, in company with his head clerk, William D. Baine and an assistant, William Paul, had been employed immediately beneath the break in the ceiling. Their attention having been drawn elsewhere at the time he considers little short of a miracle. The damage to the roof will not exceed $400. Of the stock ruined, most of which was valuable, nothing definite will be known until an investigation is made. The stock and building though covered by insurance against loss by fire, are not secured in what is known as cyclone insurance. The damage will not fall short of $1,200.

W. Hughes, brick contractor for the Baldwin building, stated to THE JOURNAL scribe that his loss is fully $900. Both the east and west third story walls thirteen feet in height, have been damaged to such an extend as to necessitate the tearing of it down to the third-floor level. The building is 140 feet in length of which, on both sides, sections 80 X 13 feet in dimensions were precipitated into the cellar. The rear thirty feet upon which a tier of joists had been laid, was not damaged to any considerable extent, although it is not now considered safe.

During the entire evening, the demolished buildings were viewed by an eager crowd, and wild and various were the estimates of the damage inflicted."

Simon's store encounters another incident of damage, a year and a half later, as reported in the *Omaha Daily Bee* on 14 May 1887:

"Damage by Water

The heavy rain of Thursday afternoon and night caused a breakage in the old sewer along the ally back of O street at Twelfth. This breakage flooded the excavation and foundation work of the Burr block to a depth of six feet, and all day yesterday two fire engines were employed in pumping it out. It was feared for a time that the foundation work already done would be ruined, and in the night fears were entertained that the four-story Baldwin block adjoining would suffer. In the excitement parties rooming in this block preferred to move out. A large number of cellars were flooded upon adjacent property. The estimated damage is $1,200, divided between A.D. Guiles, furniture, $150; S.C. Elliott, crockery, $500; E.C. Downs, furniture, $100; Rummell's grocery, $100; Baird Bros, $100, and other parties in less amount. The damage to the foundation of the Burr block is not known at the present time."

Through the years, Simon continues to be involved in community activities. The history book, "Lincoln The Capital City and Lancaster County Nebraska," by Andrew Sawyer in 1916, states in 1889 Simon is a member of the newly organized "The Old Settlers' Association" and is part of the committee of six appointed to draft a constitution for the association.

The Capital City Courier, in the 15 February of 1890 edition, reports Simon "guarded the doors and the tickets for an event where the audience is treated to imported music" played on "three Edison phonographs," described as musical cylinders sent from New York.

Even in 1890, shop owners, such as Simon, encounter problems with bad checks being used by customers!

The following article, published 1 March 1890 in the *Omaha Daily Bee*, reports:

"Under False Pretenses

John H. King, who has been working for his board at the Hub saloon, West Lincoln, languishes in the city cooler. Yesterday he came down town and espied some goods at S. C. Elliott's that he wanted, wrote a check on the First National bank for $15 and carried them home with him. When Elliott presented the check for payment the assistant cashier pronounced it no good, whereupon complaint was filed charging King with obtaining goods under false pretenses, and he was placed under arrest with the result stated."

Simon and Franc close Elliott's crockery in 1893 due to the serious economic depression that occurs across the United States. They, along with many citizens, encounter extremely difficult financial times. The couple move into Phebe Elliott's home to live with her.

Phebe Leech Elliott

Phebe Leach Elliott, Simon's sister, an 1860 graduate of Iowa Wesleyan, serves as a Professor of English Literature and Preceptors 1864-1865 at Iowa Wesleyan.

The following account, written by historian Jim McKee, for the *Lincoln Star Journal* 22 May 2011, references history of the first schools in Lincoln, Nebraska (Lancaster County):

"There is some confusion as to where the first school was taught in Lancaster County as Simon Benadom, whose cabin near Eighth and Q was later used as the Lancaster County Courthouse, said that Phoebe (sic) Elliott, for whom Elliott School was later named, taught the first school in a log cabin near Saltillo, a village near the southeast corner of Wilderness Park."

Did Phebe teach in Lincoln in the 1868 time-frame, then return to Iowa to be with her widowed mother in 1869 before relocating to Lincoln again? Was she the first of the Elliott family to live in Lancaster/Lincoln, Nebraska?

Phebe is listed in both the 1870 and the 1880 Federal Census living with her mother, Phebe Elliott, in Mt. Pleasant, Iowa. In 1870, also living with them are Lillian Vernon, age 5 and Elliott Vernon, age 3; children of Phebe and Simon's sister, Fanny Blaine Elliott, who dies at the age of 33 in 1869. As a point of interest, the children's father, Leroy M. Vernon, a clergyman, is living in Sedalia, Missouri on the 1870 Federal Census. Perhaps Phebe goes back to Iowa to help her mother with her niece and nephew.

Beginning in 1870 and ending in 1875, Phebe is a member of the Board of Trustees for Iowa Wesleyan.

Phebe and Simon's mother, Phebe Leach Elliott, dies in 1882. Within the Elliott family history, compiled by Dr. Frank Roads Elliott and Thomas Elliott, we read about Simon's mother, "Phebe made a home on the little money a circuit rider received. The salary of the Editor was better. Her husband would be away in the wilderness for six weeks on end preaching. She was intensely interested in all of his undertakings. She had good judgment, was public spirited, and took part in all women's enterprises. Her husband freely acknowledged her assistance in all he undertook.

Phebe, the practical manager, the driving force with her feet on the ground, always saving, working, looking after finances, doing the investing."

According to a letter Simon's sister, Phebe Leech Elliott, writes to the Lincoln, Nebraska newspaper, *The Nebraska State Journal*, published in the 31st December 1911 edition, she relocates from Mt. Pleasant, Iowa to Lincoln, Nebraska about 1884-1885.

While living in Lincoln, Phebe becomes quite active within the community. As previously noted, in 1884, Phebe assists Franc with her duties a Nebraska Commissioner for the New Orleans World's Industrial and Cotton Centennial.

Late March of 1887, The Prohibitionists (a political party founded in 1869) hold a convention and nominate several people for various offices within the city of Lincoln; including Phebe, who is nominated to become a member of the School Board. Interestingly, the Prohibition Party becomes the first to accept women as party members. Phebe does become a member of that School Board and is assigned to the committee tasked with "Teachers, Examinations and Salaries."

Phebe serves on the Lincoln Board of Education from 1887-1890.

The first newspaper article referring to Elliott School, named for Phebe, is found in the *Lincoln Evening Call* dated 24 Dec 1890. After thirty-two years, in 1922, the initial building housing the school is replaced by a new structure.

The real estate transactions section of the *Lincoln Evening Call* published May 1887, reports Phebe purchases from Nebraska Stock Yards Co, "lot 4, block 29, first add to West Lincoln."

Phebe is elected by the board of the "Home of the Friendless" as a delegate to represent Nebraska in the "Home of the Friendless" women's congress to be held in Washington in March of 1888. The Nebraska state Friendless home is equivalent to a senior care facility and is geared toward helping women over 50 who are alone and have no family or resources. In 1889, Phebe is listed as Corresponding Secretary of the "Home for the Friendless" at 11th and South Streets in Lincoln.

The 1889 City Directory notes Phebe living at 321 South Fourteenth Street; Simon is listed at 307 South Fourteenth. Today, these addresses in Lincoln are between 13th and 14th Streets near M Street.

In June of 1890, Phebe is one of three judges at the Cotner University's first declamatory contest. Wikipedia describes the school as beginning in 1889 as Nebraska Christian University. It was affiliated with the Disciples of Christ. No records have been located which reflect Phebe is a member of the faculty or has any other connection with the school.

The *Lincoln* Journal *Star* published 19 November 1891, reports the following about the Board of Education:

"The board met yesterday evening and went through the usual routine of business.

It was voted to have school on Friday the 27th, the day after Thanksgiving, also that the winter vacation include the 24th of December to January 4th, making eleven days including Saturdays and Sundays.

Superintendent Jones, Professor Austin, Miss Elliott and Mrs. Upton were appointed a standing committee on school exhibit at the Columbian Exposition.

The board decided that a school day should consist of five hours and that the time of opening and closing school sessions would be fixed by the superintendent.

The petition praying for the use of the First and K building for night school purposes, was referred to the superintendent with power to act. In extreme weather it was noticed that school rooms are apt to be chilly on Monday mornings owing to there being no fires for a couple of days, and as an improvement it was suggested that the janitors and superintendent unite in planning for warmer rooms on Mondays."

Phebe is a member of the Lincoln School Board again from 1892-1894.

One of the most interesting aspects about Phebe is learned from reading a letter she wrote to the Editor of the *Nebraska State Journal*, published 13 August 1892:

"A Tax Payer's Humiliation

Miss Phebe Elliott Expresses a Few Views on a Subject of General Interest.

To the Editor of The State Journal.

I believe in Nebraska and glory in being a citizen of Lincoln.

I believe in street paving, in the latest scientific appliances for city water, in paying 100 cents of every dollar of honest debts.

I have watched the building of Lincoln for twenty years with the pride of one who is a partner in its planning and construction. Having cheerfully paid my assessment of taxes during these years, recognizing the common good, as well as because of compulsion, I claim share in its ownership.

Today I have seen men who are taxpayers go to the polling booth with heads erect in the consciousness of their right to say yes or not to the issuance of over $200,000 of city bonds. I have seen men who never have paid and never will pay taxes, walk gleefully on the same errand.

I claim to have as much interest in these things as anyone in either of these classes of men and to have as much public spirit.

By the laws of this state I have no voice in these matters, being classed with the idiot, the convict and women.

As an American citizen I claim that taxation without representation is tyranny.

There are hundreds of women in this city in like position and of like mind.

It is humiliating to be ignored; it is embarrassing to as recognition; but we will not be recognized until we insist on recognition.

This condition is today's inheritance from the ages. One is not responsible for inheritances, but for ignoring the inherited disease and allowing its virus to continue to destroy the moral sensibilities. Nebraska is not without moral discernment as is evidenced by the conferring of school suffrage upon women and men with equal restrictions, thus keeping step with three-fourths of the states in the union. Let us not be laggards, but let Nebraska women and men celebrate the 400th year of this new world by inaugurating municipal suffrage - the women by asking recognition and the men by generously saying, 'certainly, there is plenty of room.'"

Lincoln, Nebraska Historical Perspective

Originally known as Lancaster in 1863, Lincoln, the capital of the state, is formed in the late 1860's. Chosen as the capital of Nebraska in 1869, it is a newly formed community during the era when Franc, Simon and Phebe live there.

During the years of Simon and Franc's residence, Lincoln reaches the following milestones:

1863:   First post office in the county established
1872:   The Lincoln Gas Light Company organizes
1874:   Post office building established

1875: Library organized by private citizens. City assumes control in 1877
1880: Lincoln Telephone Exchange organizes
1881: City Water Works begins
1885: Full-time paid fire department established
1888: New Capitol building constructed
1889: First hospital, Saint Elizabeth Hospital, founded

By 1890, the city has excellent railway connections, a good number of banks, hotels, libraries, newspapers and churches. Within the 1890 Business Directory the city boasts of a public-school system which "ranks well with that of any of our western cities." Simon Elliott's establishment for crockery and glassware is listed at 1212 O Street.

Chapter 4: 1893-1903

"Let us not be afraid to help push along the great world movements, especially those of peace and educational problems."

Franc Roads Elliott, The P.E.O. Record, 1924

Canfield and Elliott Families

Although Franc's daughter, Stella, marries into the Canfield family in 1899, it's evident over the years, beginning in 1891, the two families develop close ties and maintain a friendship.

The University of Nebraska is formed in 1869. It was in 1891 when James H. Canfield, future father-in-law to Stella, takes the position as Chancellor of the University.

From University of Nebraska University's historical background found at their website, we read of the institution's history during the 1890-1899 era: "In 1891 Lincoln was just passing from rawest frontier to civic order. There were high expectations for the city, as the habitants had unlimited energy and ambition. If trees were scarce, the newcomers planted more; if the mud was deep, they planned pavement....During the 1890s, Lincoln was a thriving community being built on excitement, hope and hard work. The University was expanding under Canfield's leadership and the public had high expectations from the faculty and administrators to produce educated students."

Within the book "Semi-Centennial Anniversary, Historical Sketches of the University of Nebraska" published in 1919, we learn more about the early days of the University. "In 1871 the University of Nebraska was emphatically the seeker and not the sought. Some of its first alumni came to be students through the advice, and indeed, in a sense, the solicitation, of its head. There being no secondary education to serve for preparation, the University was forced to administer to itself. For years in consequence its chief enrollment was its Latin School. Until the middle eighties the University of Nebraska was spoken of in legislative debates as the Lincoln High School. There was little knowledge of it in the State at large until Chancellor Canfield, in 1891-1895, carried the evangel of opportunity to every considerable town and village. College classes were now filled to repletion, and preparatory courses were discontinued."

The Canfield referenced to within the previous text, is James Hulme Canfield (1847-1909) who serves as Chancellor of University of Nebraska from 1891 to 1895. He leaves Nebraska when he becomes President of Ohio State University. According to the Wikipedia page devoted to the University of Nebraska, it is during the time between 1890 to 1895 the enrollment at the school rises from 384 to 1,500. And, per the "Historical Sketches of the University of Nebraska," Canfield's "success in filling the halls of instruction with college students was due to the plan of accrediting secondary schools, which had been put into effect in 1884." The story continues with comments from Chancellor Canfield about his efforts made just prior to his departure for Ohio. "He spoke reminiscently of his work, and mentioned incidentally that he had traveled for the University not less than 200,000 miles."

Found within the James Hulme Canfield collection, housed at the University of Nebraska, is the following biography of James Hulme Canfield, born in 1847:

"James Hulme Canfield, father of Dorothy Canfield Fisher, was born in Delaware, Ohio March 18, 1847. He lived in New York City (Brooklyn) until age 8 and then, after the death of his mother, went to live with his paternal grandmother and an aunt in Arlington, Vermont. His father, Eli Hawley Canfield, remained in New York City, minister to congregations in Manhattan and Brooklyn.

James Canfield graduated from the Brooklyn Collegiate and Polytechnic Institute in July of 1864. He attended Williams College (1864-68) and upon graduation moved west, first to Iowa, to work for various railroad companies. In 1871, he studied in the law office of Hall and Gould in Jackson, Mi., and was admitted to the bar in 1872. He remained in law practice there until 1877. Canfield married Flavia A. Camp in 1873.

James Canfield taught at the University of Kansas from 1877 to 1891. He was first professor of History and English Language and Literature and then of History and Political Science. In 1889, at his request, a position as Professor of American History and Civics was created for him. During this time, he was also secretary, and in 1889, president of the National Education Association. He remained active in the NEA through the early 1900's. Canfield left Kansas in 1891 for the position of Chancellor to the State University of Nebraska at Lincoln. In 1895, he became President of Ohio State University, resigned the position in 1899 and became Librarian at Columbia University. He remained in this position until his death.

James Hulme Canfield died March 29, 1909 after a January 1909 street car accident."

Of note, the book, "The History of Kansas" published in 1884, is authored by James H. Canfield. This is during the time, according to the biography above, he is Professor of History at the University of Kansas.

He also becomes Stella Elliott's father-in-law when she marries his son, James A. Canfield, in August of 1899. At the time of their marriage, James A. Canfield is with the Central Ohio Paper company of Columbus, Ohio. Stella is the assistant director of the gymnasium at Ohio State University.

"The Story, P.E.O. in Illinois: A History," published in 1953, states; "Between the Elliott and Canfield families there was a strong bond of friendship which was strengthened by the marriage of Stella to James Canfield."

James A. Canfield, is born in St. Joseph, Michigan and comes to Nebraska with his father in 1891. He attends the University of Nebraska at the same time as his father is Chancellor and graduates in 1895; his father's last year as the Chancellor at the University.

Charles Addison Elliott, Franc and Simon's son, graduates from the University of Nebraska with a Bachelor of Science degree in 1895 as well. While students at the University, both Charles Elliott and James Canfield are Sergeants in the Cadet Battalion of the Military Department. Charles is also a member of Phi Delta Theta.

Charles continues his education in medical school and graduates in 1898 from Northwestern University Medical School.

Stella Elliott, also attends the University of Nebraska in Lincoln. She is a member of Kappa Kappa Gamma and graduates in 1898.

The 1898 University yearbook, "Sombrero," refers to Stella May Elliott as "Lassie of the lint-white locks. Thine eye so blue and tender was one-time black." The publication lists Stella's favorite song as: *De Leader of de Company B*. The song, written and composed by Dave Reed, Jr. is dedicated to Company B., 71st Regiment New York. It is a comedic song sung by the Reed Birds.

Sometime after her 1898 graduation, Stella secures her position with the Ohio State University as Instructor in Physical Training of Women and vice-chair Associate Professor of Physical Culture. It is feasible James and Flavia Canfield are instrumental in aiding Stella obtain her position at Ohio State University. She resigns that position by January 1900.

In addition to Stella's husband, James A. Canfield, James and Flavia Canfield have a daughter, Dorothy. Dorothy is a younger sister to James by almost five years. Dorothy graduates in 1899 from Ohio State University; where her father had been appointed president in 1895.

James H. Canfield's wife, Flavia Canfield, and Simon's sister, Phebe L. Elliott, are founding members of the Lincoln Woman's Club in 1894.

Both Flavia Canfield and her daughter, Dorothy Canfield, become well-known authors.

Flavia writes stories such as: "The Kidnapped Campers: A Story of Out-of-Doors;" "The Refugee Family;" "A Story for Girls;" "Silky Buff and Dotty Jack or Price Johnnie's Chickens;" "A Trip with a Trailer;" and "Around the World at Eighty."

Becoming a very popular and prolific writer during the first half of the twentieth century, Dorothy Canfield Fisher (Mrs. John Fisher) writes the stories: "The Squirrel-Cage," "The Bent Twig," "Understood Betsy," "Home Fires in France," "The Brimming Cup," "Rough-Hewn," "Our Independence and the Constitution" and "What Shall We Do Now?: Five Hundred Games and Pastimes."

She also brings Maria Montessori's educational approach to the United States and writes the book "A Montessori Mother."

Within Julia Ehrhardt's book, "Writers of Conviction," Dorothy is further described:

"In addition to earning a Ph.D. in French from Columbia University at a time when such an accomplishment was still rare for females, and introducing Americans to the Montessori method of child-rearing through her involvement with educational organizations, Fisher also tirelessly advocated for women's rights, racial equality, children's welfare, and adult education. Simultaneously, she dedicated herself to various relief projects during World War I, relocating with her family to France to assist war refugees. In 1939, she would organize the Children's Crusade for Children, a fund-raising drive designed to aid young European war victims."

Ehrhardt continues: "Fisher cited her work as a wife and mother first and her literary career a close second, stating, 'My efforts to be a good citizen, in my personal life, really should not be given so much attention that my books, to which I have given the very core of my heart and mind, should be pushed into the background.'"

This biography continues: "as a teenager Dorothy planned on a career in music. But the small size of her hands, as well as a gradual hearing loss that began during her high-school years, forced her to abandon her dream of becoming a professional violinist."

The Canfield and Elliott families are social acquaintances while living in Lincoln. James Hulme Canfield's wife, Flavia Camp Canfield, is described as having an interest in art. This reference is made in a letter written by Simon's sister, Phebe Elliott, to Mrs. Callen Thompson and published in *The Nebraska State Journal* on 29 November of 1908.

As the first president of the Lincoln Women's Club in 1894, Phebe writes to congratulate the current president on the 14th anniversary of the Club. Within the letter she writes: "Dr. and Mrs. Canfield have built a summer home next to us. Mrs. Canfield has a large studio with sky light and does a lot of good pictures. She also copies at the Metropolitan in New York and is known as one of the best copyists there. We have many of her pictures in our home. She is certainly a genius. She has written a captivating story for children which grown people read - they sit up late at night to read. It is named 'The Kidnapped Campers.' Is published by the Harpers and dedicated to her grandsons Charley and Bob (Stella and James sons)."

From the description of Flavia artistic skills, it is plausible she and Franc find a common interest in the study of art. And, James H. Canfield's occupation as Chancellor in University education was certainly one familiar to Simon, as his sister Phebe, and their father, Rev. Charles Elliott, are well-known and accomplished in the field of education.

Elliot Family and University of Nebraska Relationships

The early years in the 1880's at the University of Nebraska are described by a student within the Semi-Centennial publication of 1919: "We devoted our time to our studies, to any outside work that we may have had, and to the interests of the literary societies, with an intensity of concentration that I am sure would make present-day professor's eyes stand out in amazement. We were everlastingly discussing questions like the tariff, the Nicaraguan canal and the immortality of the soul. When the suffrage questions came to a vote in 1882, we lined up on opposite sides not only said everything that had been put forward on the question, but after the amendment was beaten got up a respectable riot when the antis started to bury a coffin said to contain the remains of Susan B. Anthony, only to lose it to the beefier scuffs. That near riot was on the whole a very satisfactory affair. We had the band out, and made a big fire on the dirt road at Eleventh and O Streets and rowed around so much like real students that we all felt very encouraged about our rising college spirit."

That location, in 1882, Eleventh and O Streets, is directly next to Simon's store.

The *Lincoln Star* newspaper, published 12 August 1924, credits Franc as "instrumental in bringing Miss Sarah Moore to Lincoln to found the art department at the University of Nebraska."

As with any college campus, close life-time relationships are developed with fellow students and teachers.

In 1911, Charles Elliott, Franc's son, as head of the Ricketts Foundation Committee, writes a tribute to namesake of the Foundation and fellow University of Nebraska graduate, Howard Taylor Ricketts (1871-1910). This tribute gives remarkable insight into who are the people Charles, and by extension, perhaps his mother, Franc, call their friends.

Another member of this seven-member Foundation Committee is Charles H. Mayo, co-founder of the Clinic with his brother William Mayo in 1903. Four years later, in 1915, the two Mayo brothers provide $15 million to the University of Minnesota to establish the Mayo Foundation for Medical Education and Research in connection with the Mayo Clinic in Rochester, Minnesota.

Howard Ricketts, the subject of Charles' tribute, is a fellow classmate to Charles at the University of Nebraska as well as Northwestern University. Ricketts graduates from University of Nebraska in 1894 and Northwestern in 1897. As a young doctor, Ricketts devotes his life to scientific investigation and ultimately, at the age of thirty-nine he dies from typhus fever while studying its cause and mode of transmission.

Within Charles's tribute, he lists the close friends he and Howard Ricketts shared: John J. Pershing, Roscoe Pound, Dorothy Canfield, Willa Cather, and Edward P. Elliott. Charles describes them all as all being "sons and daughters of pioneers - forming a remarkable group of rather serious minded young people, as such things are judged in retrospect."

Charles' account of his college friends, who go on to lead extraordinary lives, reflects amazing insight in 1911 of the world to come.

John J. Pershing is Professor of Military Science and Tactics at the University of Nebraska from 1891-1895. While he is at the University, he attends law school and graduates in 1893. Pershing forms a drill company of university cadets. In October of 1894, former members establish a fraternal military drill organization called the Varsity Rifles. Later, the name was changed to Pershing Rifles.

Members of the Varsity Rifles include Charles Elliott, who acts as captain of Company B and is also the first captain of the company. The background of The Pershing Rifles found in the 1898 University of Nebraska yearbook, describes Charles: "He was a good commander and always had the company well in hand. The way in which he handled the company on the stage of the Funk Opera House was sufficient evidence of his ability."

The 1919 historical sketch of the University of Nebraska found in the "Semi-Centennial Anniversary Book-The University of Nebraska 1869-1919" reports:

"The outstanding feature in the history of the Military Department of the University is, it need hardly be said, General Pershing's four years' service as commanding officer of the battalion. The personality of the young lieutenant, then fresh from the Indian wars, found immediate expression in a stricter discipline and an infectious professional enthusiasm. It cannot be averred that discipline was then, nor is it now, a conspicuous quality of Nebraska Life."

The report continues,

"In 1893, Pershing received his bachelor's degree from the University in the College of Law. In the same year the Pershing Rifles were organized for voluntary additional drill. They are still in existence, destined apparently to remain a permanent part of our military organization. It may be said in general that this period of Pershing's life, with its profound impression upon the student body, foreshadowed upon a small stage his later achievements in the great field of the world's history. His name became a legendary one among successive generations of undergraduates, whose memories are usually so short. The continued residence of his family in Lincoln has tended to preserve the affection of the community for him and pride in his growing fame to a greater degree than is usually possible in so migratory a profession as that of arms."

Pershing goes on to serve as commander of the American Expeditionary Force (AEF) on the Western Front in World War I, 1917-1918. Per Wikipedia, "Pershing is the only American to be promoted in his own lifetime to General of the Armies rank, the highest possible rank in the United States Army."

Roscoe Pound, born Nathan Roscoe Pound, studies botany while at the University of Nebraska and graduates with his undergraduate degree in 1888; masters in 1889. He receives the first PhD in botany from the University of Nebraska in 1898. From 1903-1908 he becomes dean of the University of Nebraska-Lincoln College of Law. Between 1907 and 1911 he is found at the law colleges at Northwestern and then Chicago. In 1911, Pound starts teaching at Harvard and becomes dean of the Harvard Law school from 1916-1937.

Wikipedia states, "Roscoe Pound also made a significant contribution to jurisprudence in the tradition of sociological jurisprudence, which emphasized on the importance of social relationship in the development of law and vice versa. His best-known theory consists of conceptualizing law as social engineering. According to Pound, a lawmaker acts as a social engineer by attempting to solve problems in society using law as a tool."

Dorothy Canfield, as noted previously, is daughter of the 1891-1895 Chancellor of the University of Nebraska, James H. Canfield. She goes on to a career as an activist as well as an author.

Willa Cather, according to a description found at the website for the Willa Cather Foundation, is "one of the most important American novelists of the first half of the twentieth century. Seen as a regional writer for decades after her passing in 1947, critics have increasingly identified Cather as a canonical American writer, the peer of authors like Hemingway, Faulkner and Wharton."

The 1895 University of Nebraska yearbook publishes a story which Willa Cather and Dorothy Canfield take first prize together, "The Fear That Walks by Noonday." Willa is listed as one of the editors of that same yearbook. Willa and Charles attend the University of Nebraska during the same years.

To date, no relationship between an Edward P. Elliott and Charles Elliott has been established. There is, however, an Edward C. Elliott, who receives his Bachelor of Science degree in 1895 (same year as Charles) from the University of Nebraska. He obtains his Masters of Art in 1897.

This Edward C. Elliott in 1903 attends the Teachers College at Columbia University. Per Wikipedia: Edward C. Elliott devises a "unique scale to rate teachers' merit and competency." He is also credited in Wisconsin for raising "the requirements of obtaining a teacher's certification."

From 1916 to 1922 Edward C. Elliott is the first Chancellor of the University of Montana.

It's possible that this Edward C. Elliott is who Charles was referencing within his tribute to Howard Taylor Ricketts; not an Edward P. Elliott as is published in the tribute.

Franc R. Elliott: 1893-1903

Within the Elliott family history, compiled by Dr. Frank Roads Elliott and Thomas Elliott, we learn Franc, beginning in 1893, while she is living in Chicago and running a rooming house, "fitted herself to teach drawing and art in the public schools." Dr. Elliott states, "By her sheer force of ability, energy and the hardest kind of hard work, supported herself and saw Charles Elliott through his college work and medical studies. Together with Aunt Phebe she supported Stella till she too finished her college and professional training."

Franc herself provides an account for the 1917 "Iowa Wesleyan College Historical Sketch and Alumni Record" of her employment for the ten years of 1893-1903:

1893: Supervisor of Art, Freeport, Illinois, public schools

1894-1898: Supervisor of Art, Aurora, Illinois, public schools

1898-1903: Supervisor of Art, Salt Lake City public schools

Freeport, Illinois, the location of her 1893 employment, is 114 miles west of Chicago. Aurora, Illinois, the location of her 1894-1898 employment, is 42 miles west of Chicago. It is doubtful she commutes from Chicago daily for either position and likely lives in the communities where she is employed.

During the years of 1893-1903, Fran's son Charles is a student at University of Nebraska from 1891 to 1895. He attends Northwestern University Medical School 1895-1898 and afterwards has his residency at Mercy Hospital in Chicago 1898-1900. Franc's daughter Stella is a student at University of Nebraska from 1894-1898. She teaches gymnasium and physical education at Ohio State University 1898-1900. In 1899, she marries James Canfield and their first child, Charles Elliott Canfield is born in November 1900. Their second child, Robert Elliott Canfield was born in October 1903.

1894-1898: Aurora, Illinois

"The Story of P.E.O.," published in 1923, confirms Franc "was at one-time art supervisor of the public schools of

Aurora, Illinois, during which time she established the model school room." Indeed, a database available online at the Aurora Public Library, corroborates Mrs. Franc R. Elliott is a member of the East High faculty in 1896. During Franc's tenure in Aurora she develops what is referred to as "the model schoolroom."

"The P.E.O. History of Illinois," published in 1915, describes the model school room attributed as Franc's concept as: "a room properly lighted and ventilated, with hard wood floors and tinted walls on which hung pictures of merit." This history further explains, "Teachers from all parts of the country came to inspect the room. Such rooms are common today, but it was Mrs. Elliott who, by her model room, brought to school authorities a consciousness of how ugly and unsanitary school rooms had been."

Additionally, within the 1915 "P.E.O. History: Illinois," we learn Franc is the founder of the Chicago Public School Art Society, "which insures that in every public school room there shall hang at least one lovely picture, understandable to the pupils in the grade who sit before it."

According to Thomas James Riley, in his paper "A Study of Higher Life of Chicago," published in 1905, the Chicago Public School Art Society attributes Franc as the founder, who organizes the Society in 1894 to "encourage a larger aesthetic development along with the intellectual growth of the city." The study continues: "The public schools give so many children who come from ignorant or badly managed homes their first idea of what authority and a proper submission to authority signify. They are much more apt to feel that these are beneficent instead of irksome things, if the outward forms and surroundings are beautiful and attractive rather than mean or unattractive...We have yet to learn fully how much the elements of moral and spiritual character are developed by spending years early in life under the influence of good works of art, which teach beauty, patriotism, love of nature, mother-love, and reverence. Aesthetic education is one of the great moral forces of society."

Sadly, Charles A. Roads, Franc's brother, dies 22 September 1897. His death certificate indicates he dies at the Commercial Hotel in Stockton, California where he was employed as a "Hotel Man."

1898-1903: Salt Lake City Public Schools

Franc's tenure as an Art / Drawing Supervisor in Salt Lake City is quite a story!

To understand the story, it's best to start back in 1892 when a Mr. D.R. Augsburg arrives in Salt Lake City to take charge of the Drawing Program in the public schools of the city. He is also appointed as Director of Drawing in the University of Utah.

Mr. Augsburg authored "Drawing Simplified," among other books, which at the time is considered "the authorized drawing system of the Utah Territory." Utah is a territory in 1892 and acquires statehood in January of 1896.

Early in 1897, a Mr. James Taylor Harwood, Past-President, and a Mr. Edwin Evans, President, of the Utah Artists' Association, openly criticize the use of Mr. Augsburg's system for teaching art in the local schools.

Mr. Harwood, according to Wikipedia, is born in 1860 and attends the San Francisco School of Design, Académie Julian and Ecole des Beaux Arts (Paris).

In the fall of 1888, Edwin Evans, the second critic of Mr. Augsburg's system, joins J.T. Harwood and other Utah artists in Paris. Later that year, along with J.T. Harwood, Mr. Evans founds an "Academy of Art" in Salt Lake City. In 1892, he paints several murals in the Salt Lake City Latter-Day-Saints Temple as well as eight murals for the Veterans Hospital in Salt Lake City.

Evans is hired in 1898 by the University of Utah and is appointed President of the "Institute of Fine Arts" at the University. He is credited with making the University of Utah's art department possible. At the same time, Evans is reported to push for the refinement of the local art world.

The University of Utah's biography of Edwin Evans explains how the local Society of Utah exhibits, of which Harwood and Evans both serve terms as the group's president, "attracted unprecedented numbers of the local citizens."

In response to Harwood and Evan's criticism, Salt Lake City teachers decide to support Mr. Augsburg and endorse Mr. Augsburg's approach to teaching art. The teachers state they believe Mr. Augsburg should be given the opportunity to prove "to the satisfaction of practical people that said statements are not based on a thorough knowledge of the principles and aims of his system, nor on a thorough examination of its results among the majority of our pupils."

Within a week of the teachers endorsing Augsburg's system, the Salt Lake City Board of Education holds a public meeting to discuss the matter. The following newspaper account, from the *Salt Lake Herald* on 26 February 1897, details the proceedings.

> "The Augsburg System
> Is Attacked by Artists Evans and Harwood
> Its Defects Pointed Out
> Before the Board of Education Last Night
>
> Prof. Augsburg Makes a Good Defense and Has the Thorough Sympathy of His Audience - Each Side Spoke For Nearly Two Hours - The Board Will Render Its Decision Later - The Proceedings In Detail.
>
> 'Artists Harwood and Evans vs. Prof. Augsburg!'
>
> Member Colton acted as court crier, the entire board of education as judges, while 30 or 40 schoolmasters and ma'ams made up an interested audience,
>
> The trial was held in the lecture room adjoining Superintendent Millspaugh's office in the capitol building last night, and the question involved was Prof. Augsburg's system of drawing now used in the public schools of this city and which has been so viciously attacked by several of the leading artists of the city.
>
> To report all that was said would fill a 32-page edition of The Herald with matter that none but artists and a few draughtsmen would understand. Both sides talked about line of horizon, center of vision and all that sort of thing for four hours, or nearly so. The sum and substance of it all was that

Artists Harwood and Evans sought to demonstrate to the board of education that the system of drawing used in our schools as taught under Prof. Augsburg is sadly defective in principle and execution. Prof. Augsburg has published a book called "Drawing Simplified." It is the text book in use here and forms the bone of contention between the artists.

Each side was given one hour in which to present their views, but they stopped not for two hours. Mr. Evans opened preliminaries, and in doing so exhibited considerable feeling, as indeed he did throughout his extended talk.

Mr. Evans Opens.

In opening, Mr. Evans said he regretted the fact that food drawing was so little understood here, and for that reason he would be at a disadvantage, and for that reason also it would be difficult for the board to understand the importance of making a change from the present system. As a proof of the lack of knowledge of drawing in this city, Mr. Evans cited the resolution passed by a recent teachers' meeting upholding the Augsburg system and disapproving of the criticism made by the speaker and Mr. Harwood in a recent letter to the board.

After criticizing the teachers for acting hastily when passing such a resolution, the speaker said the Augsburg system not only meets with criticism at home, but also abroad, and he read the following extract from a letter over the signature of Ginn & Co., a well-known publishing house of Chicago:

'We are very much interested in your reports of the condition in the public schools in your city relative to the subject of drawing. It seems hardly possible that a city like Salt Lake is still using the Augsburg system, for it is among those least in favor with educators everywhere.'

Mr. Evans then refuted the charge that they wanted to make artists of the pupils, by saying that artists were born, not made, and that by advocating perceptive rather than conceptive drawing they but advocated a system that has a tendency to make all artistic.

The speaker's first objection against the Augsburg system was that it has done but little to aid free hand drawing. The system had not been in use five years and not a teacher scarcely can make a free-hand drawing. This was probably well, he thought, on account of the principle taught in text books. He then compared the drawings of Michael Angelo (sic), Raphael and others with those of Professor Augsburg to show the great masters treated theirs in the 'altogether' character and freedom, while the professor handles his in parts. Free-hand drawing can only be learned by free-hand treatment, a principle the Augsburg system lacks, he contended. The pupil should learn to draw first and theorize afterwards. No one ever learned to draw correctly from the study of theory.

Mr. Evans then charged the Augsburg system in its treatise on perspective to be misleading and too complicated for primary grades. As a third objection, he said the illustrations in 'Drawing Simplified' are faulty because they fail to carry out in practice what is set forth in principle. In applying the rules laid down Professor Augsburg had neither fixed a definite horizontal line nor a definite center of vision, which is to be the most important point in the picture.

Mr. Evans illustrated all his points by exhibiting drawing on a blackboard. 'The Indian tents on page 152 show the draughtman, Mr. Augsburg, up a tree!' was one of the sarcastic prods at the professor made by the speaker.

In concluding, the speaker charged that the Augsburg system does not lead the child to correct perception; does not lead the teacher or pupils to express their own ideas, but only to express copied pictures; that it turns pupils out of school empty handed and unable to draw from nature.

Professor Augsburg's Side.

At this point time was called on Mr. Evans and Professor Augsburg spoke in defense of his system as follows:

'Members of the Board of Education - Nearly ten years ago I entered the Keystone State Normal school as the director of drawing. I came fresh from the National Academy of Design in New York City. All that I knew at that time about the method of teaching drawing was what I learned in the art schools of New York and in Syracuse university where I had formerly studied.

'I tried to teach the teachers and students of the Normal school drawing as it had been taught to me in the art schools and of course I failed, though in individual cases the success was quite good. I soon learned that art school methods where the pupil began work in the morning and worked all day under favorable conditions were in no way adapted to the wants of the Normal school where drawing was only one branch among many and had to take its chances with the others. The work was not what the teachers and pupils wanted, nor what they could use after they did get it.

'I look around for other methods of teaching drawing. I tried the various systems that were then in use but with but with only a fair degree of success. They did not seem to give what we desired. At last I went to the teachers themselves and asked them what they wanted. I diligently sought for a method of teaching drawing that was adapted to graded schools. I found that neither teacher nor pupil cared for art for art's sake, nor for drawing if it was to be used as a mere accomplishment, nor would they have drawing unless you could show to them that it was of practical use to them in their work. I soon found that they wanted a drawing that they could use. A kind of drawing that would enable them to bring into the classroom a lake, a river, or a mountain; all sorts of animals, birds and reptiles; all kinds of trees, shrubs and plants, fruits, and flowers. They wanted a drawing that would enable them to show how the Esquimaux lived in the frozen regions of the north, or the savage among the tropical forests of the south, that would enable them to bring into the schoolroom the pyramids of Egypt or a Chinese pagoda. Something they could use in object lessons, and busy work, in the number and language classes, in the geography, history and physiology classes and as a handmaid to the sciences. Something that would enable them to illustrate what they saw, thought or imagined. That would enable them to open for their pupils a new field, a new world and make life wider and broader and deeper.

'After four years of study and close application to this question in the classroom I wrote the books 'Drawing Simplified,' and 'Elementary Drawing Simplified.' These books are not perfect. What text book is perfect? They would not be suitable text-books for an art school, nor were they intended to settle the thousand and one questions that arise only in the studio, but they were intended as a simple means of helping a class of people that knew little or nothing about drawing and showing them how to use it in their work. How far the success has justified the means may be shown from the fact that the book has never been sold or represented by skilled agents as other text-books have, there has never been an agent in the field to sell it that I know of and I can assure you that I have never sold a copy myself unless it be incidentally or indirectly. And yet the book has found its way into about every state in the Union, has been officially recognized and recommended by the state of New York as being in harmony with their system; it is used in the Normal schools of Pennsylvania, is officially recognized in Michigan, is extensively used in California, Colorado, Kansas, Nebraska, the Dakotas, Texas and many other states and seems to be making fair headway still.

'So much for the book, and now as to its application.

'There are two kinds of drawing, perceptive and conceptive drawing. Perceptive drawing is drawing what you see and conceptive drawing is drawing what you think. Conceptive drawing is based upon perceptive or objective drawing. It is conceptive drawing that a teacher needs far more than object drawing. If the teacher needs a tree, or a bird, or a rock, or a squirrel, it is not practical for her to go out of doors and hunt them up. Besides if she had the real object it would be better than the picture.

'The question then resolves itself into this. How can the teacher acquire both perceptive and conceptive drawing? This could not be done from object drawing alone for that trains the eye to see but not the mind to see. A person may draw objects all his life and not be able to draw even a mouse without seeing it. Just as one may know every word in the dictionary and not be able to write the simplest kind of an essay. A fine penman is not necessarily a fine writer. Neither is a good draughtsman necessarily a fine artist. There are many draughtsmen that can draw or paint objects that are placed before them beautifully and yet who are unable to compose a picture or draw the most common object conceptively, such draughtsmen are not artists, they are artisans, Michael Angelo (sic) was a poor painter but a good artist. Modern painters are far better painters than Raphael was, but he is still the greatest artist. Now, the point I wish to make is this, that in all of our school work we are constantly striving to turn perceptive knowledge into conceptive knowledge. Striving to get the principle of number out of the book into the mind of the child and make it conceptive. When do we require little children to write language stories? Just as soon as they learn the words of which the story is composed. When do we require pupils to use numbers conceptively? As soon as they have learned it perceptively. When should children begin to draw conceptively? Just as soon as they have been taught to draw an object perceptively and not before.

'The drawing in the Salt Lake City schools is both perceptive and conceptive. During the fall months when objects are plentiful and easy to procure and in the spring time when the buds, leaves and flowers are coming out, we draw from the object. All grades from the lowest to the highest draw perceptively. In the winter time when the snow covers the ground we draw from problems based on the type forms which is largely conceptive drawing. It is this kind of drawing that is going on at the present time in the city schools, and it is this kind of drawing that these gentlemen object to. They think because they do not draw conceptively that it is wrong to teach others to do so. But if this is true the laws of psychology must be changed and the books on pedagogy made over. I do not think there is any difference of opinion in the teaching of perceptive drawing, though there may be in the presentation of the subject to pupils. The real bone of contention is in teaching conceptive drawing, and this with your permission, I will take up in detail and will show you the way it is taught and the results of this teaching in the actual work of the pupil. In showing these results, the work has not been picked out, showing only the best, but the drawing of every pupil in the grade is shown you.'

The professor then proceeded to explain at great length his system and some of the teachers wanted to applaud the telling points. Master of Ceremonies Colton, however, stopped it.

When Mr. Augsburg had finished, Artist Evans closed the case for the prosecution. The members looked very wise, few of them being in possession of the first principle of drawing, and the decision is anxiously looked for."

The University of Utah's online biography of Edwin Evans reports that Evans ultimately won a three-year battle with those trying to impose "mechanical" drawing programs in public schools. Indeed, the headline of an article dated 10 June 1898 in the *Salt Lake City Herald*, claims: "Supervisor Is Not A Candidate for re-Election. This Ends the fight Between the Professor and the Utah Artists - New Man to Be Employed."

The board concludes "for the coming year a new artist, one who is in no way concerned in the controversy, would be employed as supervisor of drawing....An eastern artist will be employed to supervise the teaching of drawing in the public schools."

J.T. Harwood becomes an art instructor of the high school and Franc Roads Elliott becomes the new Supervisor of Drawing for Salt Lake City schools in September 1898.

Shortly before reporting to Salt Lake City in September of 1898, on 3 September, an article appears in a Lincoln newspaper, *The Courier*, announcing, "Mrs. S.C. Elliott and Miss Stella Elliott went to Chicago on Wednesday after spending three weeks in Lincoln with friends and relatives." The trip is taken just prior to Franc's reporting to Salt Lake City for her new position.

Another important figure in the artists political activism arena in Utah is Alice Merrill Horne. In 1889, Horne wins the Democratic party's nomination to a seat in Utah's third legislature district. According to the publication, *15 Bytes*, dated November 2008, "the largest plank in the thirty-year old's education-minded platform was the creation of a state-funded organization to foster the fine arts." Ms. Horne wins the election in November 1889 and immediately "sat down with a legislative committee consisting of Harwood, Evans, H.L.A. Culmer and Mrs. Franc Roads (who had replaced Augsburg), with an eye towards the 1899 session."

The 2008 article continues:

"Once she took her seat on January 9, 1899, Horne, almost immediately submitted her bill for consideration. By the last official day of the part-time legislature, however, the Utah Art Institute bill had still not been voted on. So as Senators and House members made their way into the halls of the Salt Lake City and County building on March 9, Horne pulled posies from a large box on her desk and pinned bouquets on the lapels of her fellow legislatures. 'This, of course, made favorable action upon the measure obligatory,' the *Salt Lake Tribune* commented somewhat sarcastically the next day, 'for what man can resist a woman's wiles.' Horne's bill had been redrafted in the Senate, and after some squabbling over the exact name of the state art collection mandated by the bill, the Senate voted 10-5 to make into law the Utah Art Institute (now the Utah Arts Council), the first state-run arts organization."

The *Salt Lake Herald* publishes the following article 16 Jan 1899 written by Franc on page 3:

"Talks By Utah Educators

Number 8

'The Function of Art in the Development of the Individual'

By Mrs. Franc R. Elliott, Supervisor of Drawing in Salt Lake City Schools

There is simple proof that we are not a fallen but an ever-rising race in the fact that an educational club is willing to discuss the proposition that beauty has a place in educating the human being. Ten years ago the proposal that art should be given a place along with the time-honored studies that minister directly to the intellect, would have been considered to say the least ridiculous; but thanks to a growing comprehension as to the part of every liberated man and women who has the welfare of the community at heart, that the true heads for deciding whether any subject shall have a place on the school programme is that the subject must be educational, not economic; that in the culture of so definitely interdependent a unity as the human mind the attempt to train only certain powers and omit the training of others, must inevitably result in the partial development even of those powers whose training is attempted. That the established school course of the past has been one-sided, and the result a warped training, educationists are ready to admit. There has been much preaching on the training of the will, though the formal intellectual studies that have claimed most of the attention of the schools, such as mental exercise in number, the technicalities of grammar, and the study of language, but after all the results have been disappointing. And has the will been trained to the extent that warrants the effort? To the student of sociology, the conclusion is inevitable that the present education is not a guarantee against selfishness, and does not direct to the best well-being of the whole community. Children's eyes and ears and hearts have a hunger that the mastery of the three Rs by the old time process cannot feed. 'Through my heart I am what I am,' exclaimed the great Pestalozzi. The thirst of the imagination must be satisfied in the school room or materialism will leave its blight on our people. The state does not do its duty to the individual or the community, if it fails to develop the best in each child. The progressive and harmonious growth of the universal community depends on the complete development of the individuals of which it is composed. The highest test of any educational system is its influence on the expansion and strengthening of the spiritual nature. In the old Greek world, they knew better than we. There the true nature of the individual was recognized, and those students which brought culture to the soul, as well as the body and intellect, were fostered. Because of this the Greeks were the most harmoniously developed of any people, and we hold as a result of their rich legacy in art, literature and mathematics. The pressing demand that the social order be spiritualized can be accomplished through the only available avenue, the public schools. The conditions of life in large centers are such that from ethical and social reasons the demand must be granted. Today the anxiety on the part of those who form the plan of study for the schools is how education may spiritualize itself. Education has come to mean the development of the whole man; the physical, intellectual and aesthetic or spiritual. It must help the individual to understand himself to justly value his kind, put himself in harmony with his surroundings, and show him how to better social conditions.

The social idea is the center of all the teachings of Froebel. If we go right to the heart of things we will find that the clay modeling, the drawing, the mat weaving, the song and the game exist primarily to relate the child to his world, for the promotion of altruism between him and his teachers, his companions and his studies. It is through this relating of things to each other and through their application in life, that the soul gains its intelligence, not through the producing of a result. Drawing in the schools has come to its present importance because preeminently it mediates, relates and unifies other studies to each other. In its several forms when rightly taught it is more altruistic than any other study. It transports and connects imagination and intellect, the actual and ideal, the objective and subjective worlds. It lends itself out to all other recognized studies, while in itself it is a thought study, generating in the mind an activity, a quality of feeling and synthetic grasp of ideas not to be attained through the most faithful devotion to literature of mathematics. The instinctive love for beauty is innate with every human and with it its natural outgrowth, expression. Side by side with this instinctive love of beauty in childhood we find the other instinctive desire of productions – the desire to create, to put outside of himself in some form the loved idea. In the crudest drawing or rudest, most absurd clay figures, seemingly lacking in every element of beauty, we must assure ourselves we see the testimony of the divine creative power. As I note this universal love for beauty and the desire to create in my continual contact with children, I am convinced that the potential artist, poet, or seer is within every child, and that the world has been made the poorer, because through our clumsy educational processes we have stifled the best until the stupid, average, or commonplace citizen is the result. The difference between the artist or poet and the rest of the world, is simply that on the one hand the mind has been trained to give attention to the things about him, until he sees in the most common things beauties of which the other never dreamed. In his immortal confession Wordsworth tells of this highly trained soul-sense when he says that the meanest thing that grows gave him thoughts too deep for tears. We wonder sometimes that men follow so meekly the leadership of demagogues. We should not wonder when the training in the schools has been so much that which makes copyists of them, too often the most successful teacher has been the one who could soonest destroy individuality. The mind is weakened by all school processes that increase the store of knowledge without, at the same time, and by the same processes, increasing the tendency to express and use the knowledge gained. It is a law that the one who never has learned to exercise self-expression forever remains a material being, always influenced from the without and subject to the will of others. Unexpressed feeling or thought is accompanied by gradual loss of mental power. The possibility of mind growth is evidenced by increasing the power of expression. No thought can be thoroughly wrought into self-hood until it has been expressed, and each new form of expression strengthens, purifies or enables self-hood – the individual. Drawing, which is one form of art, affords one of the best opportunities for self-expression, for this reason, I would make a large place for it in the schools.

Drawing trains the observation. Seeing is really an act of the mind; thousands of pictures form themselves in the eye daily that are not seen. We see only those things to which we give attention. Culture in seeing means culture of the mind, not of the eye. The power to see accurately and fully depends on the power of giving intelligent attention. No two men see exactly the same picture in the same landscape; ten men will see then different pictures from the same point of view. Each sees the picture most in harmony with his main center of interest. No finite mind can see them all; the power to see increases as the finite mind grows consciously toward the infinite. The true work of education promotes a growth of the finite toward the infinite. All true art training increases the ability to see size, color, form and relationship in the child's environment. Children do not reason very much, but they observe a great deal. The greater part of the study of drawing should be in observation, simple and direct from objects, simple, free and un-initiative work. I would lay more stress on that part of drawing that trains the eye to see and the hand to test the position and relation of actually observed objects, and less on that which makes smooth, finished, false drawings that please pupils and parents, and too often teachers. We do not write words for mere show; we want the idea, the thought, back of the expression. Drawing is nothing if it is not putting things in their right place; of what use is a line if it is not in the right place, if it means nothing, expresses nothing?

The practice of art trains the judgment – to judge, to judge vertically, to judge horizontally, to judge height and width; the greatest height and the greatest width, and every height and every width; to block in and leave blocked in; to simplify and see that there is beauty in simplicity, and that such a thing as imitation is false. Accurate observation leads to correct judgment, and comprehensive observation leads to broader thinking in regard to a greater variety of individual things and their true relationship to each other. A great portion of human thought depends on conceptions of size, form, color and relationships. Art training cultivates new and exact perceptive centers of size, form, color and relationships, and defines judgment.

One of the most important advantages of an art training comes from its usefulness in revealing the child to himself. It is an important epoch in the life of a child when it gains the consciousness of original power. While any form of self-expressions may be made the means of self-revelation, no other form exceeds this for making clear to the child the transforming truth that it was intended to be more than an imitator and follower. The highest school processes are those that do most to develop the child's originality and apply it to lines of utility and aesthetic culture. There should be no barren lives. No man accomplishes his true destiny who fails to put forth some thought or product that will make it easier for his fellow man to be happy and to attain a more complete development. Art develops originality and helps men to aid in the increase of human wisdom and power by the production of new thought, of new power and new appliances.

No teacher should ever be satisfied unless the thought implanted in the mind of the child comes forth in improved form, charged with new life and dynamic power through the child's individuality. Mistakes have been made in teaching drawing. I do not speak of it in the old sense of copying from the flat, making lines and reciting definitions. This had little or nothing in it that developed self hood. In music, the instruments, the hand, the voice and the ear have been trained, but the soul that should originate the music has been left to chance development. Even the art of oral expression has been made a process of imitation. It is doubtful whether it is possible to cultivate the habit of repeating the thoughts of others in the exact language of others without weakening selfhood and the powers of self-expression. There is no doubt whatever that we may be trained to express most admirably the thoughts of others, in the language of other, without having our powers of self-expression improved by the process. Oft-repeated drill, as mere drill, has been too much practiced as a means of defining and establishing certain powers of the mind and hand. Drill divorced from self-expression cannot retain interest, and without interest there can be no lasting benefit to the child. All true growth is from within outward. All drill for drill's sake attempts the unnatural to produce growth from without inward.

Imagination is the foundation for all the constructive arts, the builder machinist. The inventor, as well as the artist and poet, lives in the imagination. Wherever inert wood, heavy stone, dull, cold iron and steel have been made to come into life and join hands to produce a bridge, an engine, a dwelling house, a printing press, there you find human imagination at the heart of it; positive, clear and creative. Cultivating the aesthetic nature kindles the imagination and quickens the conscience. Through the imagination we put ourselves in the place of another; without imagination, there can be no sympathy for others. The imaginative man is indignant at the perpetration of a wrong and feels for the time that he is the victim of the wrong. Through imagination we become cosmopolitan; cultivating the aesthetic creates an atmosphere in which the proprieties, the amenities and virtues unconsciously grow. The latest testimony of the scientist is that the study of the harmonious and beautiful builds cell tissues in the brain that makes for the harmonious in all relations of life. One high in authority, the director of Smithsonian Institute, recently declared that if all the people could study the beautiful in color and form, prisons and police courts would soon be eliminated.

Art should form a part of the education of every child, so that he may enjoy the productions of the human mind and the beauty and uplifting suggestiveness of nature. The poet and artist interpret for us every point; Robert Browning shows us this when he makes Fra, Lippo Lippo, a middle century artist monk, say:

'For don't you mark, we're made so that we love
First when we see them painted, things we have passed
Perhaps a hundred times, nor cared to see.
And so they are better painted; better to us,
Which is the same thing. Art was given for that
God uses us to help each other, so
Lending our minds out.'

Pictures are the most subtle and far reaching of any influence. I would rather put before the children impure books than a picture in which there is false teaching. Because of this subtlety of art, reproductions of the very best examples from world-famed artists, in pictures and casts, should find a place on the walls of every school room. What could be more powerful or far-reaching in its influence upon the future citizens of this beautiful city than to have the daily influence of the best art upon the children of the schools during the most impressionable period of their lives? School rooms should be the most beautiful places on earth, far more so than churches, which are closed six days out of the seven; but, instead, the vision of the typical school room, bare as factory walls, aside from a few maps, perhaps, haunts me.

Taste is something that grows; it is not innate. To create taste requires an atmosphere of beauty. If we are to have national art; if we are to bring the beautiful into the lives of the American people, the public schools, where the children pass so much of their time, is the place to begin. One of the most practical ways in which ministers, artists, cultured fathers and mothers, women's and men's clubs, can co-operate with teachers, is the organization of art leagues for the purpose of raising money to purchase carefully selected pictures for the schools. Nothing will bring the homes and schools, which have been too long divorced, together sooner than an effort of this kind. Here in Salt Lake City, where we are so far from art centers, is this sort of effort most desirable. The children, too, should be interested and help in such a movement. The wholesome, social influence of having a hand in working together toward a beautiful object fosters a community spirit which the children cannot afford to lose.

With a word form John La Farge, in a recent address, in which he pleads for what he calls the habit of art, and I will close. He says, 'From the point of view of making more money, from the point of view of the employer and the wealth of the state, the education of children in art has been thoroughly examined, but I do not know that its general advantage to the whole state, to the protection of wealth, to the orderly arrangement of life has been sufficiently recognized. I allude to place and order, which the habit of art seems to encourage, because I care more for that side of the question. Such forms of culture help in good citizenship and in making men bear more easily with one another.'"

During 1899, Franc acts as chairman of the State Art Committee of the Federation of Women's Clubs and is appointed chairman of the committee of Awards in the exhibition prize contest held by the Utah Art Institute in December.

Franc is living in Salt Lake City and Simon is living with Phebe in Lincoln when on 17 August 1899, their daughter, Stella May Elliott marries James A. Camp Canfield in Jamestown, New York. The following is published in *The Courier*, Lincoln, Nebraska, on 2 September 1899:

"Jamestown, New York, Evening Journal, August 18th –

There was a quiet but interesting wedding in St. Luke's church on Thursday morning, the contracting parties being Mr. James A. Camp Canfield and Miss Stella M. Elliott, both of Columbus, Ohio. Miss Elliott is the assistant director of the gymnasium at the Ohio state university, having entire charge of the work with young women, and has been spending the summer at Chautauqua, taking a course in remedial gymnastics, which has just closed. Mr. Canfield is with the Central Ohio paper company of Columbus. It was more convenient for the families of both parties to meet here, so Jamestown and St. Luke's were chosen for the ceremony. The wedding party left the New Sherman house at eleven o'clock and entered the church through the chapel porch at the side. Mr. Canfield was accompanied to the chancel rail by the bride's brother, Dr. Charles A. Elliott, of Mercy hospital, Chicago. The bride followed with her mother, Mrs. Frances R. Elliott, supervisor of drawing in the public schools of Salt Lake City, Utah. Then came Mr. Canfield's only sister, Miss Dorothy Canfield of New York City, who passed to the bride's left at the chancel, and acted as the bridesmaid. Following came Mr. Canfield's mother and father, Dr. James H. Canfield, librarian of Columbia university, New York, and Mrs. James H. Canfield. In the unavoidable absence of the bride's father, her brother gave her away. The beautiful service of the Episcopal church was followed throughout; the organist of St. Luke's maintaining a soft accompaniment. The church was tastefully decorated with potted plants. At the close of the ceremony the bridal party passed to the vestry, where the parish records were duly signed and witnessed. Several photographs of the party were taken by Mrs. James H. Canfield, to be sent to absent relations and friends. The entire party was breakfasted at high noon at the New Sherman by Mrs. Elliott, after which the bridal couple left for Buffalo beyond which point their destination was not revealed. Dr. and Mrs. Canfield and daughter returned to New York on Thursday evening, and Dr. and Mrs. Elliott go back to Chautauqua for a few days – then to Chicago and the west."

Simon and Franc sell their home in Lincoln, Nebraska in December of 1899. Simon remains living with Phebe until he leaves Lincoln to move to Chicago in 1901.

In June of 1900, Franc presents an Art Committee report at the General Federation of Women's Club annual meeting held in Milwaukee.

At the end of 1900, in December, Franc, as Supervisor of Drawing in the Salt Lake Schools, attends the State Teacher's Association meeting and is reported to have "made a plea for keeping to the artistic in manual training, so that the aesthetic side of the child would be developed."

In 1901, Franc joins the National Educational Association. She remains a member, according to their 1905 report, through the 1905-1906 school year.

Franc's mother, Nancy McClure Roads, dies on 12 April 1901. Within the Elliott family history compiled by Dr. Frank Roads Elliott and Thomas Elliott we read, "Where Addison her husband was calm and serene, Nancy was the opposite temperament. She was nervous and fidgety. This had no effect on Ad (Addison), he would go calmly along while she fussed along at his side." Nancy is buried Forest Home Cemetery, Mount Pleasant, Iowa.

Three months later, a notice appears in the *Deseret Evening News*, Salt Lake City, on 11 July 1901, reporting Franc is again to be retained for the next school year at a salary of $135 per month, the same salary as she earned during the previous year.

On 6 September 1901, President William McKinley is shot. He dies eight days later. One wonders if Franc reaches out to her P.E.O. sister and another of the original seven founders, Suela Pearson Penfield? Suela, who is the President

McKinley's first cousin once removed, is living in Manhattan, New York at the time. I suspect she did.

The next newspaper notice located, published in the *Salt Lake Herald* 16 January 1902, announces Franc is "called to Mt. Pleasant, Ia., by the critical illness of her father." Another follow-on notice, dated 25 January 1902, reflects Franc, "who is at the bedside of her sick father, was been granted a leave of absence for one month without pay." No further notices are discovered referring to Franc's father's, Addison Roads, illness. It is assumed he recovers sufficiently enough for Franc to return to work. Addison lives for another four years.

The Chicago Public School Art Society lists Franc as a member in 1902. Within their directory, she lists as her residence the Windermere Hotel in Chicago. This may be where she lives during the summer holidays from the Salt Lake City schools; although, the 1900 Federal Census places Franc, Simon and Phebe living in Chicago with her son Charles at his residence.

Published 8 March 1903 is a small, one-line notice, in the *Salt Lake Herald*, "Mrs. Franc R. Elliott is quite ill and her schedule for meetings with the grade teachers is recalled till further notice."

"The Annual Report of the Utah Art Institute" for the years 1901 and 1902 is published by the Salt Lake City Star Printing Company in 1903. Within that report is a reference to Franc's work: "The Salt Lake City public schools are in advance of many larger cities, due to the supervision of Mrs. Franc R. Elliott."

By late spring 1902, Franc's life as a teacher takes a turn as she becomes the object of attack by a majority of members of the board of education; the reason? She's not of the Mormon faith.

What follow are two articles dealing with her dismissal:

21 May 1903: The Salt Lake Herald

"Wants Scalp of Mrs. Elliott
Moyle Crew Has Grudge Against Drawing Supervisor.
Fight On Over M'Kay
Board of Education Appoints Principals.

Mrs. Franc R. Elliott, special supervisor of drawing in the public schools is the special object of attack by the majority of the board of education. This fact developed yesterday afternoon, when an attempt was made to get Professor William A. Wetzell, supervisor of music, reinstated in the schools as a principal, to have charge of the music. Although Samuel M. Doxey was retained to supervise the manual training, Mrs. Elliott and Professor Wetzell were dismissed by the majority members. It now appears that, for reasons not stated, Moyle and his followers are specially desirous of getting rid of Mrs. Elliott.

The name of Mr. McKay did not appear on the list of principals who were yesterday employed for next year in the public schools by the board of education. That does not necessarily mean that he will not further be considered by the board in relations to such a position, for another special meeting is to be held in the immediate future, when his resignation will be considered. And at the same time, the board will listen to protests against his being dropped from the list of principals of the Salt Lake City schools.

Mr. McKay sent his resignation to the clerk of the board yesterday morning. It was not read at the meeting, as it was a special session, called expressly for the election of principals. Accompanying it was a long letter from the teachers of the Lowell school, who have been under the principal for some time, protesting against his removal, and wishing him unlimited success into the future.

Petitions in McKay's Favor.

Judge O.W. Powers was present at the meeting with two long petitions from Lowell school pupils and patrons, protesting against the dismissal of Mr. McKay. He was not given an audience at that time owing to the particular nature of the special session. He filed his petitions with the clerk of the board. They will be read at the meeting when the letter of resignation is brought up. At that time, the judge said he would make a few remarks upon them.

The two petitions read exactly the same, excepting that the word patron appears in one and the word pupil in the other. They read as follows:

"We, the pupils of the Lowell school, respectfully urge your honorable body to continue Mr. G.N. McKay, principal of our school, in the position which he has held so many years with signal success in the school work and to the undoubted satisfaction of the school's patrons. This spontaneous expression of our sentiments is voluntary, but none the less sincere, and in the best interests of the Lowell school district we commend to your further consideration the question of the difficulty satisfactorily filling Mr. McKay's place."

After the meeting Judge Powers said that the pupils' petition had 647 signatures, and the other 209 names. Every pupil in the school signed the first one, excepting fifteen, who stated that their parents had forbidden them to affix their names to it.

Principals are Chosen.

The board yesterday elected the following as principals for the ensuring year, the vote being unanimous:

Geo. A. Eaton	R.S. Sanborn
W.J. McCoy	J.H. Coombs
W.D. Prosser	Lucy M. Van Cott
Mary Dysart	Mrs. Mattie E. Mckay
E.S. Hallock	A.S. Martin
David A. Nelson	W.W. Barton
Miss L.M. Qualtrough	J.O. Cross
Miss Etta Powers	H.B. Folsom
Oscar Van Cott	Fred D. Keeler
Elizabeth McMillen	Mrs. Elizabeth V. Fritz
D.W. Parrat	W.S. Wallace
William Bradford	

After the report of the committee had been adopted, Mr. Moyle moved that Mr. Wetzell be employed as a principal, and that his duties include the supervision of music.

'Does not that fill a vacancy?' asked Judge Henderson.

'Yes.' Replied Mr. Moyle.

'Well, then, doesn't that stand in the way of Mr. McKay?' asked the judge.

'Not at all, because he has resigned,' was Mr. Moyle's answer.

Wetzell turned Down.

It was at this juncture that Judge Henderson said the pupils and patrons of the Lowell school wanted to be heard upon the matter of the re-employment of Mr. McKay, and suggested that the employment of Mr. Wetzell be postponed for a while. After a few other remarks had been made upon the subject, a vote was taken on the employment of Mr. Wetzell, which resulted as follows:

Ayes - Moyle, Newman and Glanque

Nays - Branting, Cummings, Chesman, Young and Henderson.

Absent and not voting - Geoghegan and Nelden

It is understood that the matter of employing Mr. Wetzell will come up at a later meeting.

By special request the board then took up the report of the committee which had decided upon the personnel of the board of examiners. It recommended the following: Miss Rosalie Pollock, Byron Cummings, William Bradford and W.L. Brown. The report of the committee was adopted unanimously.

At a meeting of the board some weeks ago, when it was recommended that Mr. Cummings be a member of that committee, there was a strenuous objection to his name appearing upon the list, and the matter was postponed indefinitely. The unanimous action of the board yesterday was a surprise to many, as it had been thought that a fight would be made against Mr. Cummings' appearing on the committee. The objection to him was not personal, but on the grounds that he, after examining the teachers, would be called upon to approve of his own work."

Another article is found 8 June 1902 in the *The Salt Lake Herald*:

> "Praises Mrs. Elliott
> Board of Education Gives a Statement on Former Supervisor
>
> When the board of education decided, a few weeks ago, that it would not re-employ Mrs. Franc R. Elliott supervisor of drawing, the suggestion was openly made in some quarters, and generally believed, that Mrs. Elliott was removed in order to make room for a teacher of the Mormon faith. This charge is denied, however, in a testimonial given by the board, which declares that financial reasons alone were responsible for Mrs. Elliott's dismissal.
>
> This is the statement:

To Whom It May Concern:

It is a matter of extreme regret to the board of education of this city that it is compelled, through unavoidable financial reasons, to permit Mrs. Franc R. Elliott to sever her connection as supervisor of drawing in the public schools of Salt Lake City.

During the past five years Mrs. Elliott has been special supervisor of drawing in our schools and she has always brought to her work the latest, best and most approved ideas on the subject. She is a lady of high culture and refinement, and her work has been characterized by her best efforts. She has been an inspiration to the teaching corps of this city. She is always helpful to the teachers, both in the class room and grade meeting, and has been untiring in her efforts to bring the teacher up to her high ideals, and in this respect she has succeeded in a marked degree of efficiency. Mrs. Elliott's worth and success as a supervisor is well known. We cannot speak too highly of the lady's qualifications and valuable characteristics. We bespeak for Mrs. Elliott continued success and an urgent demand for her services in the public schools. We are cognizant of the fact that the loss will be great to the Salt Lake City schools and desire to have Mrs. Elliott carry with her the best wishes and appreciation of the board of education of this city for her valuable and efficient service in our public schools.

Board of Education of Salt Lake City.

H.P. Henderson,

W.J. Newman,

L. Frank Branting,

Byron Cummings,

M.J. Cheeseman,

W.A. Neden,

Oscar W. Moyle,

A.G. Gisuque,

Brigham S. Young,

J.B. Moreton, Clerk"

Thus, in June of 1903, at the age of 51, Franc heads back to Chicago to live.

Simon C. Elliott and the Extended Elliott Family: 1893-1903

1894 is the year Phebe Elliott becomes the first president of the Woman's Club of Lincoln. Over the course of her lifetime, Franc appears on the membership roosters of various Women's Clubs under the umbrella of the General Federation of Women's Clubs; in Lincoln, Utah and Chicago. It is highly feasible Franc becomes active after encouragement from Phebe.

The Courier, a Lincoln, Nebraska newspaper, publishes this report on 18 May 1895: "J.J. Imhoff and S.C. Elliott have returned from Florida." The article doesn't inform the reader if the trip was for business or pleasure.

The next month, the same newspaper reports on 22 June: "S.C. Elliott and Charles A. Elliott went to Mt. Pleasant, Ia., Wednesday." As Charles graduates 12 June from the University of Nebraska in 1895, this was doubtless a post-graduation journey to perhaps visit his maternal grandparents and other Elliott family friends living in Mt. Pleasant.

In August 1898, Simon appears on a list of members of the Iroquois Club who plan to travel to Fort Sheridan, Illinois to welcome troops home from the Spanish American War. The Iroquois Club, according to their By-Laws, is a political group "guided by the principals of the Democratic party." The club is also often referred to as the Chicago Democratic Club. The club maintains rooms located in the Columbia Theater Building in Chicago.

Application for a military invalid pension is submitted by Simon in October 1898 alleging he experiences permanent disability from lumbago and rheumatism. The claim is rejected on 25 January 1899 with the notation Simon is not "notably disabled."

Once again, in October 1903 Simon, at the age of 60, applies for a partial military invalid pension, claiming he is unable to earn funds to fully support himself by manual labor due to lumbago, rheumatism, and old age. This application indicates he had been a 60-year resident of Chicago. (Although, this is an obviously a mistaken response.) On the application Simon uses his son Charles' address at 2302 Indiana Ave, Chicago. This application is accepted. Simon is paid $6 per month beginning in October 1903.

An article published 1 January 1904 in the *Nebraska Advertiser*, reports Simon being elected as Treasurer of the American Federal Union. It is unclear the date of the election, or why he's still active in a Nebraska organization if he is living Ohio in 1904.

In March of 1907, Simon again applies for a military pension based upon his age (being over 62) and his service in the Civil War. He is awarded $12 per month. On the application Simon lists his residences since the war:

Sept 1864: Mount Pleasant Iowa

1869: Lincoln, Nebraska

1901: Chicago, Illinois

1903: Columbus, Ohio

1906: Pleasantville, New York

Sometime after the economic depression of 1893, Franc and Simon move in to live with Phebe Elliott. And, while Franc procures teaching positions in Illinois and Salt Lake City, Simon continues to reside in Lincoln with Phebe. As previously stated, an article in *The Nebraska State Journal*, dated 7 Dec 1899, indicates Franc and Simon sell their home to John B. Harris. It is unknown how long the home has been for sale; remember, there is quite a severe economic depression which begins in 1892-93.

Attending a preliminary meeting for the formation of a state federation of women's clubs in Omaha, Nebraska in December 1898, Phebe Elliott is appointed to the "Committee on Place of Meeting."

Simon and Franc's son, Charles, graduates from the University of Nebraska in 1895.

Simon and Franc's daughter, Stella, attends University Nebraska and graduates in 1898.

Simon, Franc and Phebe are all listed in the 1900 U.S. Federal Census as living at 6354 Minerva Avenue, Chicago, Illinois with Charles A. Elliott, Franc and Simon's son.

Beginning in 1900, Stella and James are living in Columbus, Ohio. Their first child, Simon and Franc's grandchild, Charles Elliott Canfield is born 3 November 1900. Stella and James have a second son, Robert Elliott Canfield, born 13 October 1903.

Phebe sells her house in Lincoln about 1901 to Charles W. Bryan, who is a younger brother to William Jennings Bryan. The first census taken after the sale of Phebe's home to Mr. Bryan is the 1910 Census for Lincoln. This census lists Charles Bryan as a newspaper publisher. Wikipedia reports Charles is the publisher and associate editor of *The Commoner* 1901-1923.

During his political career Charles Bryan serves as Mayor of Lincoln (1915-1917), Governor of Nebraska (1923-1925 and 1931-1935), and is the Democratic nominee for United States Vice President in 1924. The Democratic ticket in 1924 loses to Calvin Coolidge and Charles Dawes.

Over the course of his political career, William Jennings Bryan, brother to Charles, is a member of the House of Representatives as well as a candidate for the U.S. Presidency in 1896 and 1900. William Jennings Bryan runs against

William McKinley; first cousin once removed to P.E.O. founder Suela Pearson Penfield, in both elections. In 1913, William Jennings Bryan becomes Secretary of State for Woodrow Wilson's administration.

The military pension application submitted by Simon reflects Simon's address as 443 King Ave in Columbus, Ohio on 14 Oct 1903.

Chapter 5: 1903-1915

"Mrs. Elliott, at the time of her last visit in Mt. Pleasant, was on her way east. My cousin met her in New York at a P.E.O. meeting and afterwards wrote us, 'Mrs. Franc Roads Elliott's visit gave a powerful impetus to P.E.O. She is one of the most brilliant and cultured women I have ever heard speak. I was indeed proud of our founder.'"

Quote from Clara Bird Knopp (1870-1953),
the daughter of Hiram Thornton Bird
and Mary Florence McLeran and niece to Alice Bird Babb

The 1904 Business Directory for Chicago, lists Franc as an artist living at 2302 Indiana Avenue. During the year 1904 to 1905, Charles is studying in Vienna, Austria. From the time Charles returns to Chicago, until December of 1911, Franc acts as the hostess for social occasions hosted by Charles.

Eighteen months after Franc departs Salt Lake City, the following article appears on page 3 of *The Salt Lake Tribune*, 4 December 1904. The article addresses Franc's departure from the Salt Lake City school system:

"Mormonizing the Schools
Progress Already Made Toward It.

If the Voters like it, They Can Have More of It.

Church Leaders Take Credit for Employing Gentiles When They Have No Alternative.

Returns from the school election next Wednesday will tell the Mormon hierarchy just how far it is safe to go in the demoralization of the public schools. The election of the so-called bi-partisan ticket will be taken as an endorsement of church rule. With such an endorsement, the authorities will have no hesitation in hastening the Mormonization of the schools. The defeat of their ticket will warn them to keep hands off.

The progress already made toward Mormonizing education in Salt Lake is the best indication of what may be expected if the voters express a desire for more of it.

We have seen the founder of the present school system, Superintendent Millspaugh, harassed by a Mormon minority on the School board until he gave up his work. We remember that the board, when it was controlled by broad-minded Americans, searched the United States for the man best qualified to carry on the work begun by Prof. Millspaugh. Such a man was found. Frank B. Cooper, a brilliant and progressive educator, was secured for the place. The church finally gained control. The work of the former board was undone. Mr. Cooper was gotten rid of only to find a better position at a greatly increased salary in Seattle.

With Mr. Cooper went the teachers whom the present Superintendent called 'Our best instructors.'

Board Went to Payson

Having accomplished its object, where did the Mormon board go to find a successor for Mr. Cooper? To Payson, Utah! Whom did they find? A missionary returned from Germany.

Although he was not a college graduate, the board lost no time in raising his salary to the maximum allowed by law.

It cannot be said that either Millspaugh or Cooper was hostile to the Mormon religion. Neither allowed one thing to be taught that would prejudice a child against the faith of its parents. Their sole endeavor was to develop the children under their care into reasoning, intelligent, self-reliant young Americans. From the efforts that were made to oust them it is plain that this is just what the church hierarchy does not want the children to become.

Following the missionary-Superintendent came a retinue of missionary principals bearing bishops' 'recommends' and credentials from Payson and Pleasant Grove. The best schools were reserved for teachers having these peculiar qualifications. Older and more experienced teachers were pushed aside in order that obedient Mormons might be advanced. In some instances, as in the case of W.S. Wallace of the Union School, independent Mormons were denied deserved promotion because of the stronger claims of subservient church men.

The alleged 'non-sectarian' character of the public schools under Mormon control is again exemplified in the career of the supervisors of drawing and manual training.

Gentile and Mormon Supervisor

Mrs. Franc R. Elliott, the Gentile supervisor of drawing, was let out on the plea of economy, although a teacher of unusual ability. D.W. Parratt, a Mormon, who had shown his skill in drawing by drawing a raise of salary from $82 to $122.50 in a few months was put in her place.

Samuel Doxey, a Mormon who failed as a teacher in Ogden and taught in the grades with indifferent success under Cooper, was sent to Chicago by the School Board and educated in manual training at the expense of the taxpayers.

Such is the non-sectarianism which now prevails in the public schools of Salt Lake City.

The same brand of non-sectarianism is to be found in large quantities in the organization of the School Board. Messrs. Newman, Glanque, Branting, Moyle and Thomas, with their ally Byron Cummings from the big six, who dominate all the important committees of the board. Newman, Giauque and Branting are bishops' counselors. Not one of them dares to act without the advice or consent of his bishop.

The Gentiles who have been suffered to sit on the board are absolutely powerless to stem the swelling tide of ecclesiastical domination. They have had nothing to say regarding the employment of principals and teachers. Their protests have been vain. Yet they have never opposed the Mormon faith as such. It is because of their opposition to the deteriorating influence in the schools that they have been bound, gagged and marooned by the triumphant Mormon majority.

Mormon 'Disinterestedness'

In the face of Mormon protestations of disinterred love for education it has been shown that more than $15,000 is taken annually in the form of tithes from the Superintendent, supervisors, principals, teachers and janitors of the schools. The money is never accounted for and is doubtless used for the financial aggrandizement of the 'Trustee in Trust for the

Church of Jesus Christ of Latter-day Saints.' Some of the money may be paid voluntarily, but whether it is or not, this Mormon teacher's only hope of preferment is in paying the tribute.

Thus, the teachers are deprived of means that could be used by them to good advantage in travel and self-improvement. The tithing system wrongs the public wrongs the pupil and most of all, wrongs the faithful and ambitious Mormon teacher.

Does anyone think that the avaricious leaders of any movement will overlook such a simple expedient for increasing their revenue as the employment of more and more teachers – if the voters indorse (sic) their pretensions?

Not only is the Mormon teacher expected to give of her money. The insatiable hierarchy expects her to keep a watchful eye upon the religious tendencies of the children in her charge and keep them reminded of their duties to the bishop and the church. If she be in a country school she may be required to teach the religion class which is held from two to three times a week in the school-room.

Signs and Wonders

And such stuff as is sometimes taught in these religion classes! Can the Mormon people expect their children to become great thinkers, great discoverers or broad-minded, intelligent men and women when they are taught as youngsters that the great laws which govern the universe have been and may be set aside at the instance of priest or prophet to case the pains or remove the doubts of insignificant, egotistical man?

Although there are not enough Mormon school teachers in the State to fill the vacancies which exist today, the hierarchy claims credit for the fact that 70 percent of the teachers in the Salt Lake schools are Gentiles. Although the best positions have been filled as rapidly as possible with inferior talent for purely religious reasons we are told that the School Board has nothing in view but the betterment of the schools.

When in due season 70 per cent of the teachers and all the principals are Mormons the ecclesiastics will have some new argument to prove that there is no religious preference in the board.

If the evidence already at hand be not enough to show that the hierarchy has already begun the conquest and demoralization of the Salt Lake school, what evidence is needed? Must we wait until the ruin is complete? Shall we suffer the process to go on until the evil becomes too firmly rooted to the eradicated?"

It's February 1905 before Franc's replacement is named by the Salt Lake City school board.

An article published in *The Ogden Standard* 10 February 1905 announces her replacement, Delbert W. Parratt, who supervises drawing during the intervening year, as time allowed. He is to be paid $1,500 per year. Franc's salary is reported at $1,450 per year:

"To Supervise Drawing

D.W. Parratt is Surreptitiously Chosen by Board of Education - Changes in Principals.

D.W. Parratt is now the superintendent of drawing of the Salt Lake City schools at a salary of $1,500 a year. At the last meeting of the board of education Mr. Parratt, who, since the opening of the school year, has been principal of the Fremont school, was secretly elected to the position of superintendent of drawing and will assume that position at once.

The appointment of Mr. Parratt fills the vacancy caused by the removal of Mrs. Franc R. Elliott two years ago. At that time, the reason given for the removal of Mrs. Elliott was economy, although it was freely charged at the time that being a gentile, she was removed to make room for a Mormon. Mr. Parratt is a Mormon.

At a meeting of the committee on teachers and school work of the board of education held yesterday afternoon, John A. Welch, who had been previously selected as principal of the Fremont school, announced that he would be unable to accept the position. D.R. Coombs, principal of the Utah school, was then chosen as principal of the Fremont school, and B. W. Ashton, formerly county superintendent of schools, was selected principal of the Utah school.

Miss Phebe Haidin was chosen as assistant teacher at $40 a month, to be assigned to a school later.

The action of the committee will be submitted to the board at its next meeting for approval."

Although Franc remains active in learning and attending educational events, it's unclear if she continues to teach art once she leaves Salt Lake City and returns to Chicago. According to the Elliot family history compiled by

Dr. Frank Roads Elliott and Thomas Elliott, after her return to Chicago, "she presided over Charles' home until his marriage in 1911."

Living in Chicago, Franc again immerses herself in community activities. One of these activities is becoming a member of the Woman's Club of Austin. Austin, is a neighborhood designation of Chicago west of the Loop. Cities bordering this neighborhood are Oak Park, Elmwood and Cicero. This club, identifies itself as a "Travel Club" and is associated with the Federation of Women's Clubs in the Chicago area.

Various newspaper articles published in Chicago during 1903 and 1905 allude to Franc's involvement and hostess activities within the Woman's Club of Austin. Event topics focus on history and travel such as: "Bismarck," "Emperor Frederick," "William and Empress Frederick," "French Influence in Early America" and "The Story of Pere Marquette."

The Elliott family history, compiled by Dr. Frank Roads Elliott and Thomas Elliott, reports Franc's father, Addison Roads spends his last years in Chicago, living with Franc and his grandson, Charles. As Franc doesn't leave Salt Lake City until June of 1903, it's presumed Addison moves to Chicago sometime after that date. On 21 April 1906, Franc's father, Addison Roads dies. She is named executrix of his estate. The Elliott family history narrative relates, "Addison was a very calm, serene man. He was orderly to the extreme. He was the type of man who would pile his firewood just so, with each stick in exact order and swept up every bit of wood. His nickname was 'Ad.' One hot summer day when Ad was Deputy Sheriff, all the men had their coats off and sleeves rolled up. One made a bet that when Ad showed up, he would be perfectly dressed, with his coat buttoned, he won his bet."

Four years later, Franc is found on the 1910 Census residing with her son, Charles at the same Indiana Avenue address as in 1904. At this time, Charles has a private medical practice.

The January 1910 issue of *The P.E.O. Record* reports this quote from Alice Bird Babb, "Franc always frank by name and in character, with a face full of smiles, eyes sparkling with good cheer, and greeting so cordial that you could not but be happier for meeting her, you know now as Mrs. Elliott, more serious or sedate with added years, but still always with the spirit of exuberance and gladness, delighting her friends when and wherever she meets them."

In December of 1911, Charles Elliott marries Genevieve Comstock Cole. Genevieve is sixteen years younger than Charles and the daughter of Ernest and Genevieve Cole. Interestingly, Genevieve was born 21 January 1889, exactly twenty years to the day after the founding of the P.E.O. Sisterhood.

The Cole family are from Mount Pleasant, Iowa. Within the 1880 Federal Census, Genevieve's father lists his occupation as a "Lightening Rod dealer." By 1900 and 1910, the Cole family has also migrated to Chicago; where Genevieve's father's, Ernest, occupation is reported in both census records as "stove manufacturing."

Evidence of Franc's continuing involvement in the Woman's Club of Chicago is discovered; especially as a member of the Art Committee. Her name is located within a

1910 listing of members and guests at an art reception. And, a local Chicago newspaper, *The Inter Ocean*, publishes an article in April 1913 reporting Franc is hostess for a Woman's Club of Austin event featuring the topic "The Awakening of India and the Ideals of Indian Nationalism."

Within a June 1913 *Chicago Tribune* news article, Franc is listed as a patron for a benefit performance given by girls of the Faulkner school for the benefit of the Fellowship House.

Located at 831 West 33rd Place, Chicago, the Fellowship House, is listed in the Chicago Almanac and Year-Book for 1916 as a "Social Settlement."

Franc and Simon's grandson, Frank Roads Elliott, is born 1 February 1913 to their son, Charles and his wife, Genevieve Elliott. Charles and Genevieve welcome a daughter, Margaret C. Elliott, 1 November 1914. And, a third child, Ernest Charles Elliott, is born on 15 April 1920.

The story, "P.E.O. in Illinois: A History," reports of Franc's life in Chicago, "she lived in the Windermere Hotel on the south side, near the University of Chicago where she attended lectures with much regularity, sometimes taking a full course in a subject in which she was interested."

This story also relates Franc travels widely in the United States, as well as overseas to galleries of France and Italy, pursuing her studies in art. However, thus far, the only specific record located of Franc's overseas travels, is a passenger record, reflecting travel from Southampton, England to New York in August 1914. She lists as her home address as 510 Oakwood Road, Chicago.

Franc travels to Pleasantville, New York, presumably after Simon's death, 9 May 1915, as she is listed on the New York State 1915 Census, enumerated 1 June. She is living with Jim and Stella Canfield, the two Canfield boys; Charles and Robert; as well as Phebe Elliott.

Simon C. Elliott and Extended Family: 1903-1915

Simon relocates to Columbus, Ohio in October 1903. He and his sister, Phebe, live with Stella and James (Jim) Canfield and their two children.

On a passport application, dated June 1918, Dr. Charles A. Elliott states he studied in Vienna, Austria from 1904 to 1905. It is presumed he studies medicine. However, it is yet to be discovered specifically what or at which entity Charles studies.

Simon, Phebe, Stella, Jim and the children move to Mt. Pleasant, New York in 1906. Between homes in Ohio and New York, while waiting for their house to be ready in New York, the entire group spends six months living at Canfield family summer home in Vermont.

Upon moving to Westchester County, New York in 1906, Stella Elliot Canfield's husband, Jim, and C.A. Newfang, begin Canfield Paper Company on 1 April.

According to the "Walden's Stationer and Printer" dated 10 January 1911: "The Canfield Paper Company, dealers in fine writing and printing papers, New York, have just closed their fifth year in business, and Mr. Canfield takes pardonable pride in the fact that each year has seen a larger business transacted and the house growing in reputation and favor. In these days, when so many people one meets are talking anything but encouragingly it is a real pleasure to talk with Mr. Canfield, who is exceedingly optimistic in his views on trade and general conditions, and believes that business will pan out all right. Mr. Canfield was connected with the Central Ohio Paper Company of Columbus, Ohio, for many years prior to coming to New York to establish the house which bears his name and his success in the Middle West seems to have followed him East, and is still sticking to him."

Phebe Elliott moves from Lincoln to Chicago in 1900, then to Columbus, Ohio to live with Stella and Jim. After living in Ohio for three years, she also moves to Westchester County, New York with the family. Phebe describes life for her, and Simon, within a letter from to her Women Club friends in Lincoln. News of her letter and its content is published in the *Nebraska State Journal* on 29 November 1908:

"Mrs. Callen Thompson, president of the Woman's club, has received the following letter from first president of the club, Miss Phebe Elliott, which arrived too late to be read at the birthday reunion last Monday. Miss Elliott resides at Pleasantville, Westchester county, a suburb of New York City, where she lives in the same house with 'Jimmy' Canfield and his wife, the latter being her niece, formerly Miss Stella Elliott. The letter reads as follows:

'My Dear Mrs. Thompson: I cannot tell you how much your letter rejoices me. I am delighted to be remembered by you and the club ladies. I congratulate you on your presidency of the most unique Woman's club in the country. The spirit of Lincoln women is superior to any I have met with east or west. They have enterprise and confidence with ability to sustain gracefully and positively those possessions. The two annual announcements of the club in its 'teens' make my heart beat quicker. That baby fourteen years ago was well born of it was mothered by some of the strongest women of Lincoln. I study the contents of these announcements carefully and with all kinds of emotions.

Please let the ladies know that I am still proud of them. To think that I should get your letter just at the time so many ladies in our village are asking about you! Dr. Canfield introduced you to Pleasantville a week ago when he gave a lecture on the 'Ideal Commuter's Village,' by invitation of the men's club quite accurately proposing that its spirit and method be introduced here, including both men and women. Everybody applauded.

We have a charming village, both as to people and landscape. It is the only suburb of New York that is desirable for relaxation and comfort. We are an hour's ride from the city. Stella and Jim (Mr. and Mrs. James Canfield) and I have just finished building a home together. It is a double house that does not look double, yet we each have our kitchen, dining room and living room separate, as well as front doors. My brother lives with me as he has done for a long time and we are all very happy. We have an acre of ground which we will improve. We are quite high and have wonderful views in all directions. I shall probably end my days here, but who knows? I thought that when I went to Lincoln. Well, as Browning says, 'There is clay everywhere.'

Dr. and Mrs. Canfield have built a summer home next to us. Mrs. Canfield has a large studio with sky light and does a lot of good pictures. She also copies at the Metropolitan in New York and is known as one of the best copyists there. We have many of her pictures in our home. She's certainly a genius. She has written a captivating story for children which grown people read – they sit up late at night to read. It is named 'The Kidnapped Campers,' is published by the Harpers and dedicated to my little grandsons Charley and Bob. If Lincoln folks have not seen it, I suggest that it is fine for Christmas and for the city library. The children around here come in to thank Mrs. Canfield for writing so dandy a story and talk about the characters. She has had quite an ovation.

Mrs. Canfield and I take little trips to the city together. We went to 'The Devil' together and had a great time. This play is on the 'Faust' order, but like the Faust as played in this country, leaves the devil triumphant – does not produce the second part of the poem in which Faust by repentance and service – for others regains footing and is carried to heaven by angels personating Margaret.

I forgot to say that our house is built so that we can throw our rooms together for entertainments. We have already had a few friends in for charades, ending with a little dance to sample our oak floors. I thought you would be interested.

I note the various departments of the club. The philanthropic is up-to-date. I am glad to see other departments so well kept up. Certainly, I would love to be at one of your meetings. The memory of my visit with you and the cordiality of everyone is and always will be fresh in my mind. Thank you, dear friend, for your kind words. Loving you and all,

Phebe L. Elliott."

On the 31st of December 1911, another letter from Phebe is published in the *Nebraska State Journal*:

"Dear Friends:

After fifteen years of intensely interesting life in Lincoln I began the new century in a flat in the big village of Chicago. This life, too, was intensely interesting, as is all Chicago life.

There I had the honor and pleasure of participating in the hopes and fears of a newly fledged doctor, Dr. Charles A. Elliott, my nephew, graduate of Nebraska state university and Northwestern medical college. Notwithstanding depressing circumstances always attend the first years of the practitioner in any profession, we kept brave hearts with faces toward the goal, and arrived.

After four years of this life, the necessity for it no longer existing, my thoughts turned toward Lincoln for the attachments were strong and admiration for its freedom, energy and enthusiasm unabated. In the midst of these plans I was arrested by loving and urgent voices declaring it must not be – come to Columbus and live near us. These were voices of my niece, Mrs. Stella Elliott Canfield, and my nephew, her husband, James A. Canfield. How great a thing it is to have nephews and nieces! The two baby boys were an attraction also. So, to Columbus, Ohio, we went – my brother and I. Attractive brick house just built waited for us – under the shadow of the University of Ohio – all conveniences and clean.

We cleaned the Chicago black off ourselves and the furniture and enjoyed this cozy home with room to dig in the ground after the shut-in-ness of city walls. We lived an outdoor life in that garden even in winter with our 'kettle fire,' and the babies tumbling boxes, digging, and all childish plays.

But things do not say put. In two years it became advisable for the nephew to enter the wholesale paper business in New York city. Away we all went to New York, taking a six months' residence in Manchester, Vt. On the way that pater familias and mater familias could look around for location.

We entered Manchester – a summer resort – in the midst of a February blizzard that beat Nebraska all to pieces. Great coal stoves were set up in the large summer cottage, and, absolutely comfortable, we studied the immensity of the snow-covered Green mountains, and exceptionally fine public library and other diversions – a never-to-be-forgotten experience. September 1906, brought us to Pleasantville, N.Y. It is the Green mountains in smaller scale, but milder climate. We go to the city often and in an hour. Department stores deliver here same as in the city.

This village has a population of 2,300 largely families of young men doing city business.

We arrived in the thick of a real estate boom, another repetition of Lincoln. We found a free library. A large school building, just built, is already crowded. City people are discovering us and moving in. What impresses me most is the nursing association which employs unusually competent nurses whose services are free when necessary. All classes unite in its support – Italians and Swedes included. We have a flourishing woman's club, also a woman's choral conducted by a highly musically education woman resident.

We do not live in separate houses now, but have built together a double. Each family has its own kitchen and living rooms. Three rooms can be thrown together for dancing, musicales, lectures or charades. It is built on high ground one used for Indian councils, later for Fourth of July celebrations, camp meetings and political gathers. One tree is over 300 years old. We constantly unearth local history.

The babies have grown. The twelve-year-old had just heard his first Shakespeare play.

Phebe L. Elliott."

It's interesting how the founder's lives are still touching one another in 1914.

In a passage from the 1917 "Iowa Wesleyan College-It's History and It's Alumni," page 40, we learn Mary Allen Stafford's husband, Charles, speaks upon the occasion of an oil painting of Dr. Charles Elliott, LL.D, Simon's father, being presented at the time of 1914 Iowa Wesleyan commencement:

"The school year of 1914 was dignified by two events of more than passing importance. The largest class in the history of the school, forty-four in number, were given their diplomas. At commencement time, the college was singularly honored by the presentation of an oil painting of Dr. Charles Elliott, LL. D., the great war time president of the College, and editor of the Central Christian Advocate, by his daughter, Miss Phoebe (sic) Leech Elliott. The speech of acceptance by Ex-President, Charles W. Stafford, in which, in glowing terms, he paid tribute to this great servant of the church, will long be remembered."

Simon Elliott dies 9 May 1915 in New York. He is buried at Fresh Pond Crematory and Columbarium, located in Middle Village, Queens, New York. Near to where he and Phebe were living with James and Stella.

In September of 1915, Simon's widow, Franc, expresses her frustration with the government's slow response to her application for a military widow's pension via the following letter:

"Dear Sir: I am writing you to make inquiry concerning the claim for pension due me as the widow of Simon Charles Elliott who was of Iowa infantry A 45. No of the claim is 1073601. I have been informed that the claim was allowed. Mr. Elliott died May 9th 1915. Why is the delay?

Respectfully yours, Franc R. Elliott Widow of SC Elliott"

Franc is later awarded a military widow's pension.

Chapter 6: 1915-1924

"Mrs. Elliott is the only P.E.O. Founder who might rightly be termed a resident of Illinois, having lived for thirty years in Chicago."

P.E.O. in Illinois - A History, 1955

Beginning in 1917, a variety of addresses are recorded for Franc.

The 1917 Iowa Wesleyan Alumni Record registers Franc's address as 4017 Lake Park Ave., Chicago, Illinois.

The 1918 Chicago Woman's Club directory records Mrs. Franc R. Roads as a non-resident member, with a New York City address of 27 W. 82nd Street. The reason for a New York City address is unclear. Her son-in-law Jim Canfield's business, is listed in the January 1918 "Walden's Directory of Papers" as 62-64 Duane Street, New York City. The address recorded for Franc is mid-Central Park area and not far from Columbia University. While she may attend classes at Columbia, no records exist today reflecting Franc is a student during this time frame.

As part of the passport application process for Charles A. Elliott, Franc signs documentation on 1 June 1918 to verify Charles's identity and attests she's known him for 45 years. On this document Franc lists her address as 7017 Constance Avenue, Chicago, Illinois.

According to the Elliott family history, Margaret Elliott, granddaughter to Franc, states, "My earliest memory of Nana

(Franc) was her living in Chicago with my Mother and Brother Frank during World War I, while Dad (Charles) was in Ecuador with the Yellow Fever commission."

Frank Roads Elliott, grandson to Franc, relates his memory of Franc, "After the marriage of my parents, Nana (Franc) nominally lived with us but traveled about a great deal. She attended the University of California in Berkeley several winters...summers she would take art courses at Chautauqua in the Finger Lakes Region of New York State, and in between times visited us in Chicago or Uncle Jim and Aunt Stella in Pleasantville. Always active, Franc had the mind of a statesman, speaking often against war and in behalf of equal rights and equal opportunities for women. She had also the mind of an artist, seeing beauty everywhere. Her life exhibited spirit, courage, intellect, civic interest, culture and always a forward look, the vision of thrilling things to come."

The October 1918 edition of "The University Journal - Alumni Edition (University of Nebraska)" reports: "Mrs. Franc R. Elliott, one-time art Instructor at the University, who is the mother of Dr. Charles A. Elliott, '95, did some research work at the University of California last year in Medieval history, the results of which she is planning to publish a paper treating of 'The Survival of Paganism in Christianity, as seen through art mediums, architecture, sculpture, mosaic and paintings or frescoes.'" A copy of this paper has not been uncovered.

The above references lend a hand to confirm during 1918-1919 Franc resides several months in Berkley, California while studying at the Leland Stanford University. Her studies include the causes of World War I.

According to "Out of the Heart," after completing her studies in California, Franc stops in Denver, Colorado on her way home to Chicago and attends the 1919 P.E.O. Convention of the Supreme Chapter. Mary Allen Stafford also attends and each of them speak before the Convention. Franc speaks on the "Fifty Years of P.E.O." and Mary on the "Real Meaning of P.E.O."

Remembering the recent completion of the Great War, and reflective of her recent course of study, Franc introduces a peace resolution at the 1919 Convention stating: "We P.E.O. women would join hands in any movement looking toward the abolishment of war."

In 1949, the P.E.O. Record of January-February 2015 reports, "Thirty years after Franc Roads Elliott introduced the peace resolution, the International Peace Scholarship (IPS) became P.E.O.'s third project at the Convention of the Supreme Chapter."

The 1920 Federal Census reveals Franc living with her son Charles, his wife Genevieve, and their children Frank and Margaret at 5537 Woodlawn Ave., Chicago. This address is located near the University of Chicago Medicine; and not far from Wesley Memorial Hospital where Charles is teaching and practicing medicine.

Franc Roads Elliott is known for her intellect, her dynamic personality, and her lifelong commitment to activism. In 1953, "P.E.O. in Illinois: A History," describes Franc as "an intellectual in every sense of that word. She was a constant reader, not only of the classics, but of present day books, always abreast of current-day thought.

Her conversation never ran to personalities nor weather, she had wider and more interesting topics. She was in no sense bookish nor didactic; she was always charming and delightful and when one left her it was to look forward to another meeting."

Additionally, this history recounts for us: "Dr. Garrison of the University of Chicago, speaking at her funeral summed up her life when he said, 'She was a representative of the type of woman which puts the spirit of the home into the nation, the spirit of Christ into politics and brings culture and beauty into the lives of common people.'"

The *Lincoln Star* carries this obituary for Franc 12 August 1924 on page 3:

"Early Day Art Leader is Dead

Mrs. Franc Elliott, Formerly of Lincoln, Passes Away Tuesday.

Word of the death of Mrs. Franc Elliott in Chicago Saturday was received Tuesday morning. She was prominent in art work in Lincoln from 1870 to 1885, and had many friends here. She was 72 years old.

The first classes in art and ceramics and the first firing kiln for china in Lincoln were Mrs. Elliott's, her friends recalled. She came to Lincoln a bride in 1870 and made a home in a brick house on the southwest corner of Fourteenth and M streets. Mr. Elliott conducted a china store on the north side of O street between Twelfth and Thirteenth and Mrs. Elliott had her studio above the store from about 1880 to 1885.

During her stay in Lincoln she was instrumental in bringing Miss Sarah O. Moore to this city to found the art department at the University of Nebraska. She was a member of the Hayden Art club along with other Lincoln people of that time. This club later became the Nebraska Art association. As Miss Franc Rhodes, before coming to Lincoln she was a charter member of the P.E.O. founded at Mt. Pleasant, Iowa.

In about 1885 Mr. Elliott's health failed and they went to Salt Lake City, Utah, where Mrs. Elliott was supervisor of art in the public schools for many years. Later they returned east and lived with their son, Dr. Charles Elliott of Chicago, and their daughter, Mrs. James Canfield, daughter-in-law of former Chancellor Canfield of the state university. Mr. Elliott died several years ago."

Clearly, the research done more recently doesn't match the obituary. Nevertheless, primary points of her life match and she will forever be remembered as a very independent woman; who not only was one of the seven founders of the P.E.O. Sisterhood, but was one who tirelessly promoted the positive benefits of the beauty of art to her students, her community and the world.

She raises two children of whom she could be proud.

She feels strongly about the advancement of women in society and works diligently, along with her sister-in-law, for recognition of women within her church and within the communities where she lives and teaches.

A quote found on the blog of a Kathleen C. Christensen, sums up Franc's life beautifully:

"Franc Roads had the courage to meet the challenges and to pursue the possibilities in her world. She pursued her intense interest in art throughout her life. In her professional life, her art took her into the classroom, at the high school and the college level. On a personal note, she never stopped taking art classes, to enlarge and expand her own knowledge."

Franc is not buried in Mt. Pleasant, Iowa, but, in 1952, one hundred years after Franc's birth, a Memorial is dedicated to her in Mt. Pleasant's Forest Home Cemetery. The *Mount Pleasant News*, Mount Pleasant, Iowa, publishes this story 29 September 1952 on page 1:

"Memorial to One of P.E.O. Founders Dedicated

A memorial to one of the founders of the P.E.O. Sisterhood-Franc Roads Elliott – was formally dedicated by national officers of the Sisterhood assembled in Mt. Pleasant Sunday afternoon.

A section of the program was given at the Memorial Hall in the P.E.O. Memorial building at Iowa Wesleyan with Mrs. Mabel Scurrah of Victoria, B.C. Supreme Chapter president, giving the address.

Formal dedication then took place in the quiet beauty of Forest Home cemetery where stands a newly erected granite marker to the memory of Mrs. Elliott. There Mrs. Neil Farrell Stevenson, second vice president, Supreme Chapter, of Tulsa, Okla., paid brief tribute to the founder whose memory was honored and spoke the formal words of dedication.

On the memorial stone are engraved these words under the P.E.O. Star: 'In memory of Franc Roads Elliott, wife of Simon Elliott, 1852-1924 – a founder of the P.E.O. Sisterhood.'

Mrs. Gertrude P. Tomhave, First Vice president, Supreme Chapter, of Montevideo, Minn., presided. At the Memorial Hall, Mrs. Enola Carter, chairman of the committee, presided. Mrs. Bessie R. Raney, Past Supreme President, Chicago, Ill, gave the preliminary history. Dr. J. Raymond Chadwick, president of Iowa Wesleyan, gave the prayers.

Introductions

Introductions of honored guests took place at Memorial Hall and included: Mrs. Scurrah, Mrs. Tomhave, Mrs. Stevenson.

Members of the Memorial Stone committee: Mrs. Raney, Mrs. Winona Evans Reeves, Past Supreme and State President, Chicago, Ill., Mrs. Gail Page of Ottumwa.

Trustees of the Supply Department: Mrs. Stella Clapp, Manhattan, Kan., Mrs. Beulah M. Thornton, Chicago, and Mrs. Marian Blaine, Philadelphia, Pa.:

Mrs. Gracia Linder, Committee of Ore. Memorial Hall: Miss Margaret Mohler, Executive Secretary of the P.E.O. Sisterhood, both of Mt. Pleasant:

Mrs. Turner, past state president of Missouri, Mrs. Minear, state president of Illinois; Mrs. Crawford, organizer, Mrs. Durree of Centerville, Mrs. Bernice Olson, president of Original A, and Mrs. J. Raymond Chadwick, Mt. Pleasant.

Tea At Chadwick Home

After the dedicatory service, a tea was given at the home of Dr. and Mrs. Chadwick by Chapter Original A for the visiting officials and others from a distance as well as local residents. Over 200 attended.

Mrs. Harold Garrison was in charge of the table and Mrs. H.G. Leist was in charge of refreshments, with Mrs. Paul Rathff and Mrs. Raymond Kerr assisting. Mrs. Garrison was assisted by Mr. H. F. McLaren and Mrs. Louise Clark, Mrs. Olson and Mrs. Winona Kyle, vice-president of Original A, poured.

Parlor hostesses were: Mrs. Hall Weir, Mrs. A.T. Lanning, Mrs. Richard Hall, Mrs. Dan McAllister, Mrs. Gerald Lange, and Mrs. Olan Ruble.

In the parlor, as many as could, gathered around and heard Mrs. Winona Evans Reeves, Past President, Supreme Chapter. Past President Iowa State Chapter and retired editor of the P.E.O. Record; tell of anecdotes and memories of the girlhood days of Franc Roads Elliott.

Two grandnieces of Franc Roads Elliott were present for the dedication, Dorothy Evans Carrithers of Morning Sun and Anna Evans Walker of Yarmouth.

Towns and cities, or states, represented at the dedication not previously listed, included: Barlington, New London, Brighton, Ottumwa, Washington, Iowa City, Milton, Winfield, Fairfield, Des Moines, Kansas City, Kan., and South Dakota.

The following are excerpts from the address by Mrs. Mabel Scurrah, president of Supreme Chapter, P.E.O., in connection with the dedication of the memorial stone for Franc Roads Elliott, one of the founders of P.E.O.

It is always a source of great interest to me to come to Mount Pleasant to attend the meetings of the Executive Board of Supreme Chapter but it is an especial privilege this time to be here on the campus of Iowa Wesleyan College, the Mecca for all P.E.O.'s and in the home city of the seven who in their youth gave to us the beginning of a great organization. We are here today to pay honor to all of them, but in a special way to memorialize one of them.

Today, we are remembering by a very small stone, one who was to us a great woman, who unconsciously to herself and perhaps to us here today set the pattern for P.E.O. philanthropies since her activities were in the field of education and in civic service, particularly in the advancement of women, politically and in her participation in the affairs of the church. She worked and spoke and wrote for the abolition of war as it was then called; now we speak of it as the promotion of peace, but it is one and the same thing...

The Roads family lived here in Mount Pleasant, members of her family are doubtless remembered by some who are here. During her college days, she became engaged to Simon Charles Elliott; son of Dr. Charles Elliott who was twice president is remembered as one of Iowa Wesleyan's most scholarly presidents. It is on Dr. Elliott's family cemetery lot that the Memorial stone is placed. The Roads-Elliott wedding was solemnized in 1872 here in Mount Pleasant. Two children were born to them, Charles A. and Stella. After a few years the young people moved to Lincoln, Neb., where Mr. Elliott was in the mercantile business and Franc, true to her tradition took graduate work. Their son, Dr. Charles Elliott, a widely known physician, was head of the School of Medicine, Northwestern University. Their daughter, Stella, married James Canfield, brother of Dorothy Canfield (Fisher). None of the family are now living. Mrs. Elliott's activities and achievements are a part of P.E.O. history.

Mrs. Elliott worked for seventeen years to have women admitted to the General Conference of the Methodist Episcopal church, which is the law-making body of that denomination...

She was the first to suggest and to carry out the plan of a model school room, a room with hard-wood floors, tinted walls, on which were hung beautiful pictures; a room properly lighted and well ventilated...

She was an art supervisor in the public schools of Lincoln, and was the first instructor of art in the Nebraska State University, where her two children were educated."

Extended Elliott Family

The United States enters World War I in April 1917. A year later, in March of 1918, the first outbreak of Influenza is reported: at Camp Funston, Fort Riley, in Kansas. This was the first case in America of what was a world-wide pandemic. Today the illness is referred to as the 1918 flu or the Spanish Flu.

An estimated 10% - 20% of those infected die between March 1918 and late in 1919.

Meanwhile, in June of 1918, Franc's son, Dr. Charles Elliott, is appointed to membership on a Rockefeller Foundation International Health Board Commission. This

Commission is sent to Guayaquil, Ecuador to "investigate the presence of yellow fever and allied diseases." Guayquil was deemed the center of the yellow fever epidemic.

Within the 1918 "Annual Report of the Rockefeller Foundation" is the following summary:

"Personnel of Commission to Guayaquil and Subjects Studied:

The investigation was entrusted to a Commission composed of Dr. Arthur I. Kendall, Dean of the Northwestern University Medical School, Chairman, Dr. Hideyo Noguchi, of the Rockefeller Institute for Medical Research, Dr. Mario G. Lebredo, of Cuba, Dr. Charles A. Elliott, and Mr. Herman E. Redenbaugh. The Commission, provided with laboratory equipment, arrived in Guayquil on August 2. It was extended the courtesy of an official reception and was given every facility for the conduct of its investigations. The results of its activities have been reported in the form of four separate studies, as follows:

1. A Sanitary Survey of the Republic of Ecuador, by Drs. Kendall and Lebredo;

2. A Bacteriological Study of Yellow Fever, by Dr. Noguchi;

3. A Clinical Study of Yellow Fever, by Dr. Chas. A. Elliott, and Supplementary Report by Dr. Lebredo;

4. A Chemical Study of Yellow Fever, by Mr. Redenbaugh.

Dr. Noguchi succeeded in isolating an organism, to which he has given the name of Leptospiraicteroides, which is the apparent cause of yellow fever. At the end of 1918 much work was still required to demonstrate that the true etiologic agent had been discovered, but the prospect for success is most encouraging. If the germ of yellow fever has been discovered it will still further simplify the problem of eradicating the seed-beds of yellow fever; and upon the successful completion of that task, the disease should disappear from the earth."

Dr. Noguchi continued his research and in 1921, the Rockefeller Foundation's Annual report states that the "experience with Naguchi's vaccine and serum indicated that the former when properly administered affords a marked protection against attacks of yellow fever, and that the latter if it is used on or before the third day of the onset of the disease reduces the mortality in a striking way."

However, in 1926, a paper published raises the possibility that the L. Icteroides identified by Dr. Noguchi, might not be the causative agent of yellow fever. The Foundation quietly stops distribution of the vaccine.

Phebe Elliott, on 20 Dec 1919, writes a letter to the *Sunday State Journal* in Lincoln, Nebraska. It is published in the 4 Jan 1920 edition. Her reflections about woman's suffrage and the World War recently ended, are quite touching:

"Phebe L. Elliott

Pleasantville, N.Y., Dec 20,

Friends of the City with Prophetic Name: I am still a western woman, have known Lincoln from its infancy for fifty years, even before its railroad arrived. This first knowledge was thru my brother, Simon C. Elliott, of its pioneer group. He has passed on leaving me the sole survivor of my father's and mother's family. Nothing relating to Nebraska is foreign to me. A Nebraska head line instantly arrests my attention. You are my people. You are making good your prophetic name, facing always the sunrise.

It is a pleasure to have a message from Will Owen Jones, to know that he is still at his post and remembers me. The Journal would not be the same without him. I hear that Mrs. Jones is still pursuing music. Admirable!

With the opening of the century, after fifteen years in Lincoln, I moved to Chicago, in four years moved to Columbus, Ohio, in two years more to the good village of Pleasantville, New York, an hour away from New York City. Thirteen years a New Yorker, I enjoy the distinction of being Aunt Phebe to the village. Young and old do me that honor and I enjoy the enlarged family relationship. I still enjoy to the utter most the home which with James A. Canfield and Mrs. Stella Elliott Canfield, both Nebraska products, I united in building thirteen years ago. It is a haven of rest to us all and wonderful in its possibilities in our eyes. The greatest treasure is their two children who are my grand nephews, names Charles Elliott Canfield and Robert Elliott Canfield in honor of the House of Canfield and the house of Elliott, both six footers, Charles, 19 years, a sophomore at Dartmouth and Robert, 16 years, a junior in the Pleasantville High school, with his eyes on Dartmouth and as good as gone after his brother. What shall we do then? No boy, no noise. We will see.

It is a privilege and joy to watch their unfoldment of body and yet more marvelous mental and spiritual unfoldment. We also grow thru the charm of their growth. They have opinions and are foot-ball enthusiasts. The father is as much a kid over foot-ball as his sons. Discussions are abundant and technical abundant.

Mr. Canfield is increasingly like his father, Dr. James H. Canfield, former chancellor of the University of Nebraska. He is head of the Canfield Paper company, wholesale, New York City, and takes part in all village movements, served two terms on its board of education, is active in Y.M.C.A., boy scouts, and social life. Stella Elliott Canfield, as afore-time, is energetic. You think of her as energy. Her wise moulding of her two sons I do not attempt to report. She, like their father craves the best for them. Largely she has yielded to the desires of the high school basket-ball girls to act as referee in absence of their regular official. This temporary change from the usual community service refreshes by contact with sweet young girls also remember her service in that line in the U of N assisting Mrs. Anne Barr Clapp in gymnasium. Blessed be the automobile. It is a member of our family. Without it I would not get away from the ground. We sound its praise daily. It is a dear old servant. We pat it and love it. It is jolly to see that 'everybody is doing it.' A semi 'shut in' the auto is my only chance. So many willing hands in the family and by neighbors to furnish frequent trips any time in the day or night thru the absorbing Westchester hills. They never become monotonous. I have the sunniest room in the house and finest outlook over the hills and far away. Four large windows with large glass to east and southeast and south, blinds run up to the tip top, day and night you have a communion with the infinite in the great outdoors. From your bed, you see a sky full of stars move past, Orion, Pleiades, Mercury, the glorious morning star thru November, splendid as a sun. Let the moon be companion, shine in on the floor and walls, make shadows all over the room. Try it, practice it. No chance for blue devils. Doing this deep in your consciousness is the healing and preserving knowledge that your travel in companionship of the stars in their courses and underneath are the everlasting arms. Sitting here as in a watch tower I take note of our crazy world writhing in one of its spells – part of its purification, getting rid of poisoned blood. Painful process. New life must follow I will believe. Men will always fight but later with superior forces. Not with bombs destroying the physical but with weapons of the intellect guided by the spirit of good will. This will take ages but they are but a day, any hour. It is a cosmic process. Let us not be children insisting on instant fulfillment of demands.

The silver anniversary of the Lincoln Woman's club was to me sacred. A day for retrospect. I observed it with high inspiration, visualized the pageant, the social side and the rest, and tried to measure the value of the large number of admirable women who must have engaged from time to time to sustain and advance so broad and numerous an institution. It has more than realized the hopes of those who planted the seed.

The soil was more fertile than we knew. The number of members dazzling. It does not necessarily mean strength yet it shows life energy, faith and is desirable.

Remember, ladies, the greatest joy is, yet to build. Let us go on.

The unanimous voice of the Nebraska legislators is ratifying the federal suffrage amendment calls out gratitude and pride. It was my privilege during the suffrage campaign in New York state to associate with some of the leaders who did most of the moving.

The Hudson is six miles away. In the auto, we could attend many of the river town conventions, also in the city. It was an education. Team work was good and the spirit sisterly. Politicians were so surprised at the almost perfect state organization they said so! Said it was better than theirs and adopted parts of it. We have been received cordially at the polls and by the parties. We miss our genial Dr. Anna Howard Shaw, the courageous, who has passed into the unknown. She rose, like Abraham Lincoln, from abject poverty by her own exertions to world recognition was the intimate of rulers and leaders. Queens of England, Belgium, and Italy recognized her war help.

We have Mrs. Flo. Winger Bagley, another Lincoln product, and her family for next neighbors. Her husband, Dr. William Bagley, is professor at Columbia. We count them part of our family.

With salutations from the Canfields and Elliotts.

Phebe L. Elliott."

Phebe's date of death remains undiscovered by this author. However, her death is presumed to occur sometime between January 1920 and September 1928.

Phebe is found listed on the 1920 Federal Census, enumerated January 1920, living at the same address as Jim, Stella and their two sons.

The next mention of Phebe found is within a newspaper article, dated 28 September 1929. The article is a report of an interview with Jim and Stella Canfield conducted during a visit to Lincoln. Within the interview, Jim and Stella mention Phebe is deceased.

Chapter 7: After Franc

"P.E.O.'s should ever keep their eyes forward, to note the possibilities of the future rather than to dwell on the achievements of the past."

Franc Roads Elliott, early 1900's

Franc and Simon's Son: Dr. Charles Addison Elliott (1873-1939)

From the Elliot family history, compiled by Dr. Frank Roads Elliott and Thomas Elliott, Franc's great-grandson:

"Charles graduated Lincoln public schools in 1891, became a Guide at the World's Columbian Exposition in 1893, and graduated with a BS from the University of Nebraska in 1895. While at the University he was a Cadet with the Pershing Rifles in 1894 and 1895.

Charles started his medical studies at Northwestern University Medical School, graduating in 1898, served his internship and residency at Mercy Hospital 1898-1899. He began private practice starting in 1900. In 1904, he decided to travel to Vienna, Austria for a year of studies, returning in 1905. He served as attending physician at Cook County Hospital 1905-1910, Wesley Hospital from 1905-1929 and Chief of Medical Staff at the new Passavant Hospital from 1929-1939. He was Head of the Medical Department at Northwestern University Medical School from 1919-1939. Charles was appointed to International Health Board, Yellow Fever Commission and in 1918 sent to Ecuador by the Rockefeller Foundation. In 1927, he made a lecture tour of

Australia and New Zealand, under the auspices of the American College of Surgeons. Dr. Charles Elliott was elected Vice President of the American Medical Association (AMA) in 1928-1929 and a Fellow of American College of Physicians in 1929. In 1933 he acted as Physician-in-Chief to the Peter Bent Brigham Hospital in Boston."

From the "Quarterly Bulletin Northwestern University Medical School, 1940 Spring," pages 61-62:

"It is fitting that the first issue of the new series of the Quarterly Bulletin of Northwestern University Medical School should speak, even at the risk of repetition, of the life and work of these men whom the medical world still mourns. Having spent their entire professional careers as members of the faculty of Northwestern, the story of their rise to eminence is, in a sense, a saga of our school. Dr. Charles A. Elliott was born in Lincoln, Nebraska, on March 6, 1873. He received his Bachelor of Science degree from the University of Nebraska in 1895 and three years later was graduated from the Northwestern University Medical School. After serving as resident physician at Mercy Hospital in Chicago for two years, he engaged in the general practice of medicine. Soon, on the advice of Dr. Christian Fenger, he gave this up and, after studying for a year in Vienna, returned to Chicago to enter the specialty of Internal Medicine. He was appointed to the faculty of the medical school as a Clinical Assistant in Medicine and he rose to become Professor and Chairman of the Division of Medicine, the position he held at the time of his death. On his return from Europe he began a five-year period as attending physician at the Cook County Hospital and for twenty-five years he carried on an active teaching and private service at Wesley Memorial Hospital. Since 1929 he headed the medical staff at Passavant Memorial Hospital. He was a founder of the Institute of Medicine of Chicago, the Chicago Society of Internal Medicine, and the Central Society for Clinical Research. He was a member of the Association of American Physicians, a fellow of the American College of Physicians, and in 1927 was honored by the American Medical Association in being elected its Vice President. In spite of recurrent manifestations of cardiovascular disease, he chose to carry on his work and did so until he became bed-ridden shortly before his death."

Franc and Simon's Daughter-in-Law: Genevieve Comstock Cole Elliott (1889-1965)

Ann Elliott Weisberg, great-granddaughter to Franc and Simon, remembers her grandmother, Genevieve, "Nana was addicted to mystery stories and double solitaire. She was always happy to entertain children and grandchildren at the summer house at Long Beach, Michigan City, Indiana. Many 4th of July picnics were spent with bonfires and rockets."

Another great-granddaughter, Jane Elliott, reminisces about her grandmother, "She married and appeared unhappy in early life. She was not prepared to be a mother, and I'm quite sure we all owe gratitude to Mary Augustine, who largely played the mother role for my dad (Bud), at least. I don't really remember much about her, except that in my very youngest years, she like to go walking with me, in her 'grandma' shoes, back in the woods in Long Beach. She knew a lot about plants and trees, and always passed on a lot of nature lore.

I remember understanding as a small child that it was Marg's 'job' to come back to Michigan City and take care of

Nana. By the time they moved to Edgewood in the late 50's, Nana really needed her assistance. Sometime just before they moved to Edgewood, Nana developed insulin dependent diabetes. I know Marg devoted a lot of time to managing her meals, but also remember Nana making a career of sneaking candy and other foods she wasn't supposed to have. She went to live in the Beverly Shores Nursing Home around 1960, and pretty much declined. She lit herself on fire (sneaking cigarettes). She sustained burns over much of her body and died in Passavant Hospital a few days later."

Franc and Simon's Grandson: Frank Roads Elliott (1913-1974)

From the Elliot family history, compiled by Dr. Frank Roads Elliott and Thomas Elliott, Franc's great-grandson:

"As a child, Frank lived on the South side of Chicago and attended the University of Chicago Elementary and High School. He was expected to follow his father's footsteps and studied medicine. He graduated from Exeter, Dartmouth and Northwestern University Medical School earning BM, MD, and MS degrees. In 1936, he married Alice Louise Erdman.

His practice was interrupted by World War II, during which he served with the Naval Reserve in the Pacific as a medical officer on an attack cargo ship. During the war while Frank was training with the Seabees, Frank's family lived with his wife's parents, Lee and Ella Nolde Erdman, in Reading, Pennsylvania.

In 1946 the family moved to Glencoe, Illinois on Chicago's North Shore. Frank started an Internal Medical Practice with offices in Chicago and the North Shore. He was on the teaching facility of Northwestern Medical School and a staff member of Passavent Memorial Hospital. He developed a blood coagulation machine used widely at that time.

His favorite hobbies were his wood shop and model railroading and circus models. He got involved with Boy Scouts with his twin sons, Thomas and Charles, helping with first aid meets and enjoyed camping. He shared bird watching with his first wife, Alice. She died in 1959.

With his second wife, Elizabeth (Bunny) he enjoyed antiquing. He was more interested in the boxes of tools under the tables than the antiques on the tables. In later years, he enjoyed a conifer garden in the back yard, his own arboretum with whatever he could get to grow in the Illinois climate.

His ashes were scattered in the back yard among his evergreens."

Franc and Simon's Granddaughter: Margaret C. Elliott (1914-1996)

From the Elliot family history, compiled by Dr. Frank Roads Elliott and Thomas Elliott, Franc's great-grandson:

"Margie was intellectual and studies came easy. She could have skipped several grades but it was not appropriate in those days to have a younger sister in the same grade so she was shipped off to private school. She graduated from Dana Hall, Wellesley, Massachusetts in 1932, University of Wisconsin with a BS in both Physical Education and General Science in 1936 and Northwestern University Medical School with a BM in 1940 and a DM in 1941. She went into pediatrics practice in Seattle, Washington until after World War II when she returned to Michigan City, Indiana to care for her Mother, Genevieve Cole Elliott.

Margie was an Artist, having studied at the Chicago Art Museum. She exhibited locally with modest success. She prided herself in keeping physically fit and active. She played golf as an amateur and was ranked in the Indiana State Women's Tournament.

Margie was a true Renaissance Woman in a time when independence and professional women where not encouraged or appreciated. She particularly enjoyed the Natural Sciences and Anthropology. She went on many amateur filed research studies with the Museum of Natural History, Chicago, with trips to the Galapagos Islands, Ecuador, Peru and up the Amazon River. While in Florida she continued field studies such as shelling and fossil hunting.

Margie made time to enjoy life."

Franc and Simon's Grandson: Ernest Charles Elliott (1920-1993)

From the Elliot family history, compiled by Dr. Frank Roads Elliott and Thomas Elliott, Franc's great-grandson:

"Ernest, Bud, attended Mercer Academy, a Military school in Pennsylvania and then the University of Wisconsin. Bud's major achievement in these years were fast cars, power boats and motorcycles. He also devoted nearly a semester to build a model of the Pioneer Limited that won a prize from Model Railroading Magazine. His life changed when he went into the Army Air Corps in late 1941. He served in Texas and Hawaii and was discharged in late 1945.

Bud graduated with a degree in Mechanical Engineering (BSME) from University of Wisconsin in 1946. He moved to Michigan City in March 1948. He hated working but loved the opportunity to use his imagination. He spent his spare time watching the stars, building models of the moon and enjoyed computers."

Franc and Simon's Daughter: Stella Mae Elliott Canfield (1843-1947)

From the Elliot family history, compiled by Dr. Frank Roads Elliott and Thomas Elliott, Franc's great-grandson:

"Stella attended University of Nebraska and became Assistant Instructor of Physical Education. During the time that James H. Canfield was Chancellor of the University (1891-1895), the Canfield and Elliott families were close friends. Later, when Dr. Canfield was Chancellor of Ohio State University, Stella was head of the Department of Physical Education for Women there. In 1899, she and Dr. Canfield's son James A. Canfield were married and moved to Pleasantville, New York."

Stella and Jim build a house with Simon and Phebe and remain in Mt. Pleasant until sometime after 1923, the last record of that residence. By 1928 we find Stella and Jim retired and living in Arlington, Vermont. Over the next several years, Stella and Jim live in Vermont, as well as Florida. Stella dies in 1947 in Florida. She is buried in Vermont.

Franc and Simon's Son-in-Law: James A. Canfield (1874-1959)

Jim, after retiring from Canfield Paper Company and after Stella's death in 1947, appears to remain living in Vermont.

Many years later, Ann Elliott, daughter to Stella's nephew, Frank Elliott, attends Bennington College in Arlington, Vermont and remembers Jim Canfield coming to pick her and her college roommate up from school to take them for an outing. She remembers thinking that she wished he didn't drive quite so slowly, as she was sure they were bound to have an accident!

Jim dies 29 May 1959.

Franc and Simon's Grandson: Charles Elliott Canfield (1900-1973)

From *New York Times*, 9 May 1973

"Charles E. Canfield, board chairman of the Canfield Paper Company of New York, died Sunday at Putnam Memorial Hospital, Bennington. He was 72 years old and had lived here since his retirement in 1963.

Mr. Canfield, who had represented New York paper merchants in negotiations with labor unions was president of the Paper Merchants Association of New York in 1951-52.

He rose through the ranks in the family concern, which was established by his grandfather (sic) James A. Canfield and Carl A. Newfang in New York in 1906. He joined the company in 1923, a year after he graduated from Dartmouth College, and became a sales man and then manager of the Philadelphia office.

Between 1942 and 1946, Mr. Canfield served in Washington as a non-salaried civilian on loan to the War Procurement Board, controlling the procurement and allocation of printing papers.

In 1946, he succeeded Mr. Newfang, who was retiring, as president of Canfield and held that post until 1963, when he became chairman.

His aunt was the popular novelist, Dorothy Canfield Fisher.

Mr. Canfield leaves his wife, Dorothy; a son, James; two daughters, Mrs. Molly Falk and Mrs. Nancy Dominie, and a brother, Robert E. Canfield. "

Franc and Simon's Grandson: Robert Elliott Canfield (1903-1980)

From *News-Gazette*, Lexington, Virginia, 19 March 1980.

"Robert E. Canfield, 77, of Rt. 1, Buena Vista, a retired official with the paper industry, died Sunday in Stonewall Jackson Hospital.

Mr. and Mrs. Canfield moved here in 1972 from New York City and built their modern house, Lee's View, with a commanding view of the valley and mountains.

Born in Columbus, Ohio, Mr. Canfield grew up in New York, where his father founded the Canfield Paper Co., and graduated from Dartmouth College and Harvard law school.

He was a partner in the New York law firm of Wise, Whitney and Parker and successor firms from 1934 to 1956. From 1957 until his retirement in 1968 he was president of the Printing Paper Manufacturers Association.

Since his retirement he had continued to take an interest in the Canfield family property at Arlington, Vt.

He is survived by his wife, Althaea Kindlund Canfield, a son, a daughter and six grandchildren.

A memorial service will be held Thursday at 4:30 pm in the chapel of the Lexington Presbyterian Church by Dr. David W. Sprunf. Burial will be at a later date in Mount Hope Cemetery at Hastings on Hudson, N.Y."

Roads and Elliott Ancestors

Pedigree Chart for Frances Elizabeth Roads

Addison Roads
- b: 28 Feb 1825 in Hillsborough, Highland, Ohio, USA
- m: 07 Mar 1849 in Hendricks, Indiana, USA
- d: 21 Apr 1906 in Chicago, Cook, Illinois, USA

George W. Roads
- b: Abt. 1785 in Rockingham County, Virginia, USA
- m:
- d: 25 Oct 1852

Mary Elizabeth Boyd
- b: 27 Apr 1794 in West Virginia, USA
- d: 30 Jan 1873

Frances Elizabeth Roads
- b: 10 Feb 1852 in Henry County, Iowa, USA
- m: 06 Jun 1872 in Mt Pleasant, Henry, Iowa, USA
- d: 09 Aug 1924 in Chicago, Cook, Illinois, USA

William McClure
- b: 18 May 1795 in Botswurt, Virginia, USA
- m: 15 Jan 1815 in Tennessee, USA
- d: 27 Oct 1850 in Hendricks, Indiana, USA

Nancy McClure
- b: 13 Aug 1824 in Rogersville, Hawkins, Tennessee, USA
- d: 12 Apr 1901 in Mt Pleasant, Henry, Iowa, USA

Frances Rose
- b: 10 Apr 1796 in Tennessee, USA
- d: 29 May 1850 in Hendricks, Indiana, USA

Pedigree Chart for Simon Charles Elliott

Simon Charles Elliott
- b: 23 Dec 1843 in Muskingum, Muskingum, Ohio, USA
- m: 06 Jun 1872 in Mt Pleasant, Henry, Iowa, USA
- d: 09 May 1915 in New York, New York, USA

Charles Elliott
- b: 16 May 1792 in Glenconway, Donegal County, Ireland
- m: 14 May 1822 in Salem, Mercer, Pennsylvania, USA
- d: 06 Jan 1869 in Mount Pleasant, Henry, Iowa, USA

Phebe Leech
- b: 26 May 1803 in Salem, Mercer, Pennsylvania, USA
- d: 14 Sep 1882 in Mount Pleasant, Henry, Iowa, USA

John Elliott
- b: 1759 in Donegal, Ireland
- m: 25 Aug 1781
- d: 16 Mar 1809 in Ireland

Frances Blaine
- b: 01 May 1764 in Ardara, Donegal, Ireland
- d: 28 Mar 1845 in Mill Creek, Coshocton, Ohio, USA

John Boyd Leech
- b: 29 Nov 1767 in York, Pennsylvania
- m: 25 Nov 1788 in Little York, York, Pennsylvania, USA
- d: 01 May 1864 in Mercer, Pennsylvania, USA

Jane Morrison
- b: 16 Jan 1769 in York County, Pennsylvania
- d: 16 Oct 1841 in Sugar Grove, Mercer County, Pennsylvania, USA

Photographs

William McClure Home: Courtesy of Jane Elliott

Addison Roads:
Courtesy of Tom Elliott

Nancy McClure Roads:
Courtesy of Tom Elliott

Addison Roads Home: Courtesy of Jane Elliott

Nancy McClure Roads and Frances Roads:
Courtesy of Jane Elliott

Frances Elizabeth Roads:
Courtesy of Tom Elliott

Charles Arthur Roads:
Courtesy of Jane Elliott

Rev. Charles Elliott:
Courtesy of Jane Elliott

Phebe Leech Elliott:
Courtesy of Jane Elliott

Simon Charles Elliott:
Courtesy of Jane Elliott

Fannie Elliott Vernon:
Courtesy of Jane Elliott

Simon and Franc Elliott Home Lincoln Nebraska: Courtesy of Jane Elliott

Simon C. Elliott:
Courtesy of Jane Elliott

Franc R. Elliott:
Courtesy of Tom Elliott

Charles Addison Elliott:
Courtesy of Jane Elliott

Stella May Elliott:
Courtesy of Tom Elliott

Stella May Elliott and Franc R. Elliott:
Courtesy of Tom Elliott

O Street Lincoln Nebraska 1870-1880: Courtesy Jim McKee and Lincoln Star Journal

Nebraska Exhibit New Orleans Fair 1884:
World's Industrial and Cotton Centennial Exposition
Stereographic Views, Mss. 4206,
Louisiana and Lower Mississippi Valley Collections,
LSU Libraries, Baton Rouge, Louisiana.

Charles A. Elliott:
Courtesy of University
of Nebraska, Sombrero, 1898, page 237

Stella M. Elliott 1898:
Courtesy of University
of Nebraska, Sombrero, 1898, page 37

Stella Elliott Canfield: Courtesy of Jane Elliott

Dr. James Hulme Canfield:
Courtesy University of Nebraska

James A. Canfield:
Courtesy of Jane Elliott

Dorothy Canfield Fisher:
Courtesy of The Ohio State
University Library Archives

Dr. Charles A. Elliott and Franc
R. Elliott:
Courtesy of Jane Elliott

Letter from Franc to Bureau of Pensions Department 1915:
Courtesy of Sharon S. Atkins

Genevieve Cole Elliott:
Courtesy of Tom Elliott

Frank Roads Elliott and Dr.
Charles A. Elliott:
Courtesy of Jane Elliott

Frank Roads Elliott and Dr.
Charles A. Elliott:
Courtesy of Tom Elliott

Ernest Charles Elliott – Margaret
Cole Elliott Dr. Charles A. Elliott:
Courtesy of Tom Elliott

Phebe Leech Elliott: Courtesy of Tom Elliott

First Elliott School Lincoln Nebraska 1918:
Courtesy of Jim McKee and Lincoln Star Journal

Franc R. Elliott:
Courtesy of Tom Elliott

Franc R. Elliott:
Courtesy of Tom Elliott

Dr. Charles A. Elliott:
Courtesy of Tom Elliott

Dr. Frank R. Elliott:
Courtesy of Tom Elliott

Dr. Margaret C. Elliott:
Courtesy of Tom Elliott

Ernest C. Elliott and Olga W. Elliott: Courtesy of Jane Elliott

Olga Wallmo Elliott:
Courtesy of Jane Elliott

Dr. Frank R. Elliott:
Courtesy of Jane Elliott

Dr. Margaret C. Elliott:
Courtesy of Tom Elliott

Dr. Frank R. Elliott:
Courtesy of Jane Elliott

Dr. Frank R. Elliott and Alice Louise Erdman Elliott:
Courtesy of Jane Elliott

Bibliography

1. 45th Iowa Volunteer Infantry Regiment. Wikipedia. Web. Accessed 22 Aug 2017.
2. "A Little Twister." *Nebraska State Journal* (Lincoln, Nebraska), 14 Sep 1886:8.
3. Andreas, A.T. *History of the State of Nebraska*. Chicago, Illinois. 1882.
4. *Annuals of the Chicago Woman's Club for the first forty years of its organization, 1876-1916*. Chicago, Illinois. 1916. Page 284.
5. *Annals of Iowa*, Volume 17, No. 7. Jan 1931. Web: Abandoned Towns, Iowa Gen Web History.
6. "Appointed for County." *Katonah Pioneer* (Katonah, New York), 13 Jun 1919.
7. "A Tax Payers Humiliation." *Nebraska State Journal* (Lincoln, Nebraska), 13 Aug 1892:8.
8. Becque, Fran."P.E.O. Founder Kansas State Convention Sigma Chi." *Fraternity History and More*. Web. Accessed 6 July 2017.
9. "Board of Education." *Lincoln Journal Star* (Lincoln, Nebraska), 19 Nov 1891:2.
10. *Book Reviews: A Monthly Journal Devoted to New and Current Publications*. New York, New York. January 1900. Page 280.
11. "Business Notices." *The Nebraska State Journal* (Lincoln, Nebraska), 02 May 1882: 4.
12. "Busy Day for the State Association – Election Occurs Today." *The Salt Lake Herald* (Salt Lake City, Utah), 28 Dec 1900:5.
13. "Can Two Societies Exist?" *Nebraska State Journal* (Lincoln, Nebraska), 11 Oct 1893:8.
14. "Capital City Grist." *Omaha Daily Bee* (Omaha, Nebraska), 4 Jan 1890: 4.
15. "Charles E. Canfield, Chairman of Family Paper Concern, Dies." *New York Times*, New York, New York. 9 May 1973.
16. Charles W. Bryan. Wikipedia. Web. Accessed 21 Aug 2017.
17. "Charter and By-Laws of the Iroquois Club of the City of Chicago." Chicago, Illinois. 1882.

18. "Chautauqua." *Nebraska State Journal* (Lincoln, Nebraska), 2 Oct 1888:8.

19. Clap, Stella, *Out of the Heart a Century of P.E.O. 1869-1969*. Des Moines, Iowa: P.E.O. Sisterhood, 1968.

20. Clara Chipman Newton. Wikipedia. Web. Accessed 3 Aug 2017.

21. "Club Department." *The Courier* (Lincoln, Nebraska), 25 Dec 1897:5.

22. *Collection Summary James Hulme Canfield Papers, Special Collections*, University of Vermont Library. Web. Accessed 17 August 2017.

23. "Color Line Won't Down." *The Sun*, New York, New York. 9 June 1900:8.

24. Cross, Anson K., *Drawing in the Public Schools. A Manual for Teachers*. Boston, Massachusetts. A.K. Cross, 1893.

25. "Damage by Water." *Omaha Daily Bee* (Omaha, Nebraska), 14 May 1887:5.

26. Davis, Eric. *United States Timeline 9200 BC to 2015*. http://hopes-and-dreams.net/ . Accessed 10 June 2017.

27. "D.R. Augsburg, L.P." *The Daily Utah Chronical* (Salt Lake City, Utah), 5 Jun 1893:6.

28. "Dr. J.H. Canfield, Of Pleasantville, Dies." *Katonah Times*, (Katonah, New York), 2 Apr 1909.

29. "Drought and Depression in 1890s Nebraska." *Nebraska State Historical Society Blog*, (Web) 23 May 2017.

30. "Early Day Art Leader is Dead Mrs. Franc Elliott, Formerly of Lincoln, Passes Away Tuesday." *The Lincoln Star* (Lincoln, Nebraska), 12 Aug 1924:3.

31. "Educational." *The Salt Lake Herald* (Salt Lake City, Utah), 8 Mar 1903:16.

32. Edward C. Elliott. Wikipedia. Web. Accessed 23 Aug 2017.

33. "Edwin Evans." J. Willard Marriott Library, The University of Utah. Web. Accessed 6 Jul 2017.

34. "Edwin Evans." Wikipedia. Web. Accessed 6 Jul 2017.

35. Ehrhardt, Julia. *Writers of Conviction: The Personal Politics of Zona Gale, Dorothy Canfield Fisher, Rose Wilder Lane, and Josephine Herbst.* Columbia, Missouri. 2004.

36. Elliott, Charles A. *Howard Taylor Ricketts 1871-1910*, Ricketts Foundation Committee (Chicago, Illinois). 1911.

37. Elliott, Earl S. Jr. *Elliott Family History 1816-2003, Fannie Blaine Elliott.* Lincoln, Nebraska. 2004. Page 32, 113.

38. Fine, Eve, *Mary Thompson Hospital*, Encyclopedia of Chicago (www.encyclopedia. chicagohistory.org).

39. "Former Nebraskans Write to the Old Home Folks." *Sunday State Journal* (Lincoln, Nebraska). 4 Jan 1920:40.

40. *Forty-First Annual Announcement of the Chicago Woman's Club 1917-1918.* Chicago, Illinois. 1917. Page 173.

41. "Frances Willard (1839-1898)." 6 Methodist Women Who Fought for The Vote. United Methodist Church (www.umc.org). Accessed 19 Sep 2017.

42. Furnas, Robert. *Report of Robt. W. Furnas, United State Commissioner for Nebraska at the World's Industrial and Cotton Centennial New Orleans.* Lincoln, Nebraska. 1885. Page 16.

43. Gale Research." Panic of 1893." 1997. http://www.encyclopedia.com/history/united-states-and-canada/us-history/panic-1893 . Accessed 15 Sep 2017.

44. Hanson, Dr. Henry, Personal Diary." Yellow Fever in South America and the Failure of the Noguchi Vaccine." 1924-1937. http://exhibits.hsl.virginia.edu/hanson/yellow-fever-in-south-america-and-the-noguchi-vaccine/ . Accessed 28 Aug 2017.

45. Haselmayer, Ph D., Louis A., Revised by Garrels, Elizabeth E., and Nemiz, Carol, *The P.E.O. Sisterhood at Iowa Wesleyan College.* Mount Pleasant, Iowa. 2005.

46. History of Hendricks County, Indiana. Chicago, Illinois. 1885. Page 646.

47. History of Nebraska. Wikipedia. Web. Accessed 8 Aug 2017.

48. *History of Nebraska Methodism*. www.usgennet.org/usa/ne/topic/religion/MEChurch/hmec/pages/honm0517.htm. Web. Accessed 10 Aug 2017.

49. P.E.O. Sisterhood, Illinois Chapter. *P.E.O. in Illinois – A History, 1903-1953*. Mendota, Illinois. 1953. Pages 13-15.

50. "Indorse Augsburg." *The Salt Lake Tribune* (Salt Lake City, Utah), 7 Feb 1897:4.

51. Inspiration Home Designs. *Wedgwood Buying Guide*. www.ebay.com. 2009.

52. Iowa Department of Cultural Affairs. *Iowa and the Underground Railroad*. Undated. Page 24.

53. *Iowa Normal Monthly, Historical – Souvenir*. Dubuque, Iowa. February 1889. Page 297.

54. James Taylor Harwood. Wikipedia. Web. Accessed 14 Aug 2017.

55. Jeffrey, Herbert Norton. *Iowa Wesleyan College – Its History and Its Alumni 1842-1917. Memories*. 1917.

56. John J. Pershing. Wikipedia. Web. Accessed 22 Aug 2017.

57. Johnson, Susan." Beginnings of P.E.O.–Iowa Wesleyan History." 2005. Web. Accessed 5 Oct 2017.

58. "Knights of Honor." *The Nebraska State Journal* (Lincoln, Nebraska), 17 Dec 1881:4.

59. "Labor Union Elects Officers." *The Nebraska Advertiser* (Nemaha City, Nebraska), 1 Jan 1904:6.

60. "Martha Canfield Library Aims to Foster Dialogue on Fisher Debate." *Bennington Banner* (Bennington, Vermont), 8 Aug 2017:1

61. McKee, Jim." A look back at Lincoln's oldest schools." *Lincoln Journal Star* (Lincoln, Nebraska), 22 May 2011. Web. Accessed 21 Aug 2017.

62. McKee, Jim." A look back at Lincoln's oldest schools." *Lincoln Journal Star* (Lincoln, Nebraska), 3 Mar 2013. Web. Accessed 21 Aug 2017.

63. McGee, Jim." Downtown Lincoln in 1875." *Lincoln Journal Star* (Lincoln, Nebraska), 2 Jul 2016. Web. Accessed 21 Aug 2017.

64. Marquette, Rev. David. *A History of Nebraska Methodism First Half-Century 1854-1904*. Cincinnati. 1904. Page 531.

65. Marshall County, Iowa. Wikipedia. Web. Accessed 25 Jul 2017.

66. Marshalltown, Iowa. Wikipedia. Web. Accessed 25 Jul 2017.

67. "Memorial to One of P.E.O. Founders Dedicated." *Mount Pleasant News* (Mt. Pleasant, Iowa), 29 Sep 1952:1.

68. Memphis and Charleston Railroad. Wikipedia. Web. Accessed 22 Aug 2017.

69. Moran, Tom, *Iowa in the Civil War*. Iowa Pathways. Iowa Public Television. Undated.

70. "Mormonizing the Schools Progress Already Made Toward It." *The Salt Lake Tribune* (Salt Lake City, Utah), 4 Dec 1904:3.

71. Mott, David C., *Abandoned Towns, Villages and Post Offices of Iowa*, Annals of Iowa, Vol 17, No 7, January, 1931.

72. "Mr. and Mrs. J.A. Canfield Visit Here." *The Evening State Journal and Lincoln Daily News* (Lincoln, Nebraska), 28 Sep 1928:1.

73. "Mrs. Elliott's Art Reception." *The Lincoln State Journal* (Lincoln, Nebraska), 5 Jun 1884:8.

74. "Mrs. Franc R. Elliott." *The Salt Lake Herald* (Salt Lake City, Utah), 4 Mar 1900:15.

75. National Educational Association, *Yearbook and List of Active Members of the National Educational Association July 1, 1905 – June 30, 1906*, Winona, Minnesota. 1905.

76. National Park Service. National Register of Historic Places Program, *The Home of the Friendless*. Web. Accessed 10 Aug 2017.

77. *New Orleans Centennial Exposition Stereoscopic Views*. World's Industrial and Cotton Centennial Exposition Stereographic Views, Mss. 4206, Louisiana and Lower Mississippi Valley Collections, LSU Libraries, Baton Rouge, Louisiana. www.lib.lsu.edu. Web. Accessed 17 Aug 2017.

78. "News of Nebraska." *Omaha Daily Bee* (Omaha, Nebraska), 2 Sep 1884:4.

79. "News of Nebraska." *McCook Weekly Tribune* (McCook, Nebraska), 18 Dec 1884:2.

80. "Notable Utah Women Mrs. Franc R. Elliott." *Deseret Evening News* (Salt Lake City, Utah), 24 Feb 1900:14.

81. "Notices." *Burlington Weekly Hawk-Eye* (Burlington, Iowa), 18 Mar 1865:4.

82. "Notices." *The Nebraska State Journal* (Lincoln, Nebraska), 19 Oct 1876:4.

83. "Notices." *The Capital City Courier* (Lincoln, Nebraska), 6 Apr 1889:2.

84. "Notices." *The Courier* (Lincoln, Nebraska), 3 Sep 1889:7.

85. "Notices." *Capital City Courier* (Lincoln, Nebraska), 5 Oct 1889:1.

86. "Notices." *Capital City Courier* (Lincoln, Nebraska), 15 Feb 1890:3.

87. "Notices." *The Courier* (Lincoln, Nebraska), 12 Apr 1890:7.

88. "Notices." *The Capital City Courier* (Lincoln, Nebraska), 15 Apr 1890:8.

89. "Notices." *Capital City Courier* (Lincoln, Nebraska), 30 Aug 1890:8.

90. "Notices." *The Capital City Courier* (Lincoln, Nebraska), 11 Apr 1891:8.

91. "Notices." *Capital City Courier* (Lincoln, Nebraska), 21 May 1892:8.

92. "Notices." *The Courier* (Lincoln, Nebraska), 18 May 1895:4.

93. "Notices." *The Courier* (Lincoln, Nebraska), 22 Jun 1895:4.

94. "Notices." *The Courier* (Lincoln, Nebraska), 3 Sep 1898:7.

95. "Notices." *The Inter Ocean* (Chicago, Illinois), 24 May 1903:30.

96. "Notices." *The Inter Ocean* (Chicago, Illinois), 24 Aug 1905:20.

97. "Notices." *The Inter Ocean* (Chicago, Illinois), 26 Apr 1913:4.

98. Ohio History Connection. *Wyandot Indians*. Ohio History Central www.ohiohistorycentral.org. Assessed 10 Aug 2017.

99. "Open Campaign for War Savings Stamps." *Katonah Record*, (Katonah, New York), 1 Feb 1918.

100. *Our History-Chautauqua Institution*. www.chq.org . Accessed 16 Aug 2017.

101. "Personal Mentions." *The Salt Lake Herald* (Salt Lake City, Utah), 16 Jan 1902:2.

102. *Portrait and Biographical Album of Henry County, Iowa*. Chicago, Illinois. 1888. Page 517-518.

103. "Praises for Mrs. Elliott." *The Salt Lake Herald* (Salt Lake City, Utah), 8 Jun 1903:5. Web.

104. Prohibition Party. Wikipedia. Web. Accessed 9 Aug 2017.

105. *Quarterly Bulletin of Northwestern University Medical School, Spring*. 1940. Volume 14:1. Pages 61-62.

106. "Real Estate Transfers." *The Nebraska State Journal* (Lincoln, Nebraska), 7 Dec 1899:6.

107. "Regarding Stella Elliott and James Canfield Wedding." *The Courier* (Lincoln, Nebraska), 2 Sep 1899:7.

108. Reeves, Winona Evans, *The Story of P.E.O.*, Supreme Chapter of P.E.O., First Edition 1919.

109. Reeves, Winona Evans, *The Story of P.E.O.*, Supreme Chapter of P.E.O., Second Edition 1923.

110. Riley, Thomas James. *A Study of the Higher Life of Chicago*. Chicago. 1905.

111. Ripley, George and Dana, Charles, Editors. *The New American Cyclopedia: A Popular Dictionary of General Knowledge*. Volume VIII 1863. Page 105.

112. "Robert E. Canfield." *News-Gazette* (Lexington, Virginia), 19 Mar 1980.

113. Robert Wilkinson Furnace. Wikipedia. Web. Accessed 6 Aug 2017.

114. Roscoe Pound. Wikipedia. Web. Accessed 22 Aug 2017.

115. Rossiter, Shawn. "Flowers & Feuds. The Utah Arts Council's Early Years." *15 Bytes,* Artists of Utah ezine. November 2008. Page 1.

116. "Salt Lake News." *The Ogden Standard* (Ogden, Utah), 10 Feb 1905:8.

117. "Samuel L. Howe." *Mount Pleasant News* (Mount Pleasant, Iowa), 11 Nov 1972.

118. Sawyer, Andrew J. *Lincoln The Capital City and Lancaster County Nebraska*. Chicago, Illinois. 1916.

119. "School Board Meets." *The Salt Lake Herald* (Salt Lake City, Utah), 25 Jan 1902:3.

120. "School Girls to Give Twelfth Night on Lawn." *Chicago Tribune* (Chicago, Illinois), 4 Jun 1913:11.

121. "School Profile: Elliott Elementary." *Lincoln Journal Star* (Lincoln, Nebraska), 1 Aug 2010.

122. "School Teachers Chosen." *Deseret Evening News* (Salt Lake City, Utah), 11 Jul 1901:5.

123. *Semi-Centennial Anniversary Book-The University of Nebraska 1869-1919*. Lincoln, Nebraska. 1919.

124. "Semi-Centennial of Church." *New Rochelle Pioneer*, New Rochelle, New York. 6 Oct 1906.

125. "Silver Wedding." *Omaha Daily Bee* (Omaha, Nebraska), 9 Dec 1882:8.

126. "Some Social Events." *Lincoln Evening Call* (Lincoln, Nebraska), 24 Dec 1890:8

127. "Studied Art One Summer." *The Salt Lake Herald* (Salt Lake City, Utah), 11 Feb 1905:8.

128. "Supervisor Is Not a Candidate For Re-Election." *The Salt Lake Herald* (Salt Lake City, Utah), 10 Jun 1898:8.

129. "Talks by Utah Educators." *The Salt Lake Herald* (Salt Lake City, Utah), 16 Jan 1899:3.

130. "The City." *The Nebraska State Journal* (Lincoln, Nebraska), 22 Oct 1880:4.

131. "The Club Woman." *The Nebraska State Journal* (Lincoln, Nebraska), 29 Nov 1908: B2.

132. The Paper Record. *Walden's Directory of Papers*. January 1918. Page 19B.

133. The P.E.O. Record. January-February 2015. Des Moines, Iowa. 2015. Page 31.

134. The P.E.O. Sisterhood, *Illinois State Chapter, P.E.O. In Illinois: a History, 1953*. Illinois State Chapter of the P.E.O. Sisterhood. 1953. Pages 13-15.

135. The Rockefeller Foundation Annual Report 1918. Concord, New Hampshire. Pages 83-88

136. "The Story of the 'Old Mill' As Told by A Howe." *Mount Pleasant News* (Mount Pleasant, Iowa), 11 Sep 1936. Web. Accessed 31 Aug 2017.

137. *The University Journal, Alumni Edition*, Volume 14, Issue 4. Lincoln, Nebraska. October 1918. Page 19.

138. The Willa Cather Foundation. Web (www.willacather.org). Accessed 22 Aug 2017.

139. "They Take the Lead!" *Capital City Courier* (Lincoln, Nebraska), 6 Apr 1889:4.

140. *Thirty-Fifth Annual Announcement of the Chicago Woman's Club*. 1911-1912. Page 117.

141. "To Supervise Drawing D.W. Parratt is Surreptitiously Chosen by Board of Education." *The Salt Lake Herald* (Salt Lake City, Utah), 10 Feb 1905:8.

142. "To the Ladies of Omaha and Douglas County." *Omaha Daily Bee* (Omaha, Nebraska), 2 Sep 1884:4.

143. "Topics of Teachers Busy Day for the State Association Election Occurs Today." *The Salt Lake Herald* (Salt Lake City, Utah), 28 Dec 1900:5.

144. "Troops on the Move." *The Inter Ocean* (Chicago, Illinois), 26 Aug 1898:2.

145. "Under False Pretenses." *Omaha Daily Bee* (Omaha, Nebraska), 1 Mar 1890:6.

146. University of Nebraska, *Sombrero*, 1898. Page 37, 237.

147. University of Nebraska, *Sombrero*, 1895. Page 238.

148. University of Nebraska. Wikipedia. Web. Accessed 10 August 2017.

149. *Walden's Stationer and Printer*, Volume 34, Part 1. 10 Jan 1911.

150. *Walden's Stationer and Printer*, Volume 39. 25 Apr 1916. Page 96.

151. "Wants Scalp of Mrs. Elliott." *The Salt Lake Herald* (Salt Lake City, Utah), 21 May 1903:8.

152. "Well Known Former Residents Send New Year Greetings." *The Nebraska State Journal* (Lincoln, Nebraska), 31 Dec 1911:42.

153. William Jennings Bryan. Wikipedia. Web. Accessed 21 Aug 2017.

154. Williams, Sandy. "Samuel L. Howe." *Mount Pleasant News*. (Mt. Pleasant, Iowa), 11 Nov 1972.

155. "Women's Christian Association." *Omaha Daily Bee* (Omaha, Nebraska), 17 Oct 1891:1.

156. "Woman's Work in Clubs." *The Nebraska State Journal* (Lincoln, Nebraska), 31 Dec 1899:18.

157. "Woman's Work in Clubs." The Tribune (McCook, Nebraska), 30 Oct 1884:2

158. *Yearbook and List of Active Members of the National Educational Association for the Year Beginning July 1, and Ending June 30, 1906.* Winona, Minnesota. 1905. Page 232.

About the Author

Sharon S. Atkins

Passionate about genealogy research and assisting people to discover their personal connection to history, Sharon thrives on writing the stories behind real people. Using her thirty-seven years of genealogy research experience, Sharon is also the author of several genealogy-related educational publications.

She is a popular speaker, founder of Its' All Relatives, a board member of APG (Association of Professional Genealogists), a member of NAGS (Northern Arizona Genealogy Society), NEHGS (New England Historical and Genealogy Society), and GSBC (Genealogical Society of Bergen County, New Jersey).

Sharon and her husband Tom live in Prescott Valley, Arizona.

Made in the USA
Middletown, DE
30 December 2023

47007683R00128